Taking Godly Care of I

Stewardship Lessons in Physical Health

by Anna Layton Sharp

Illustrated by Russ Flint

Carson-Dellosa Christian Publishing
Greensboro, North Carolina

It is the mission of Carson-Dellosa Christian Publishing to create the highest-quality Scripture-based children's products that teach the Word of God, share His love and goodness, assist in faith development, and glorify His Son, Jesus Christ.

". . . teach me your ways so I may know you. . . ."
Exodus 33:13

For Mom,
Who thanklessly made all my sandwiches on whole wheat bread
and never allowed breakfast cereal containing marshmallows to enter our kitchen.
I'm sorry for saying that you weren't cool like other moms.
You're the coolest mom and editor a girl could have!

Credits
Author: Anna Layton Sharp
Editor: Carol Layton
Illustrator: Russ Flint
Cover Design: Annette Hollister-Papp
Cover Illustration: Russ Flint
Layout Design: Mark Conrad

Unless otherwise noted, all Scripture is taken from the HOLY BIBLE, NEW INTERNATIONAL VERSION Copyright © 1973, 1978, 1984 International Bible Society. Used by permission of Zondervan Bible Publishers.

Scripture on the back cover and Scriptures marked THE MESSAGE are taken from The Message. Copyright © 1993, 1994, 1995, 1996, 2000, 2001, 2002. Used by permission of NavPress Publishing Group.

Scriptures marked GNT are taken from the Good News Translation—Second Edition, Copyright © 1992 by American Bible Society. Used by permission.

Scriptures marked NCV are taken from the *International Children's Bible®, New Century Version®*, copyright © 1986, 1988, 1999 by Tommy Nelson™, a division of Thomas Nelson, Inc. Nashville, Tennessee 37214. Used by permission.

Scripture quotations marked NLT are taken from the Holy Bible, New Living Translation, copyright © 1996. Used by permission of Tyndale House Publishers, Inc., Wheaton, Illinois 60189. All rights reserved.

Scriptures marked NASB are taken from the NEW AMERICAN STANDARD BIBLE®, Copyright © 1960,1962,1963,1968, 1971,1972,1973,1975,1977,1995 by The Lockman Foundation. Used by permission.

Scriptures marked KJV are taken from the King James Version. Public domain.

ISBN 1-59441-081-X

Introduction

Christian schools have a wonderful opportunity—and responsibility—to teach body stewardship. Poor nutrition and a sedentary lifestyle are causing what some pediatricians call an epidemic of juvenile obesity, diabetes, and high blood pressure. Students spend about half their waking lives in school. Using this time wisely can reverse dangerous health trends, and form positive habits for kids to take home. Use the following ideas to create a classroom where students honor God with their bodies.

Contents

Teacher tips . . .
For a health-minded classroom

Use the following ideas to create a classroom where students honor God with their bodies!

We know that kids may take or leave what we say, but they naturally tend to do as we do. "Set an example for the believers" (1 Timothy 4:12) by giving up vending machine fare, packing healthy lunches, even arriving to school winded from your bike ride!

Set a healthy body image attitude for the classroom. Be careful not to focus on your own or others' appearances. Even a simple comment to another teacher, such as "You look great! Have you lost weight?" perpetuates the ideal of thinness and the idea that how we look is of utmost importance. It's easy to put all the blame on television and magazines, but the adults in students' lives do have greater influence.

Class parties don't have to be sugar fests. Instead of frosting, decorate cakes with edible flowers like honeysuckle, violets, chamomile, or nasturtiums. Substitute chips and dip with tortilla chips with guacamole or salsa. Find creative ways to make healthy foods more fun. Arrange carrots, cucumber slices, and other veggies into a self-portrait. Who gets to eat the teacher's nose? Instead of soda, liven up juice with ice, a shot of club soda, and chopped fruit.

Make school events active. When at all possible, go outside for a science lesson, put a concept to song and dance, play math games in the gym, break up sit-down lessons with calisthenics or stretching.

Limit homework, and whenever possible, make after-school assignments active. Have students take walks with their families, go on a nature scavenger hunt, tend a small garden, have a pretend blackout night with no television or computer, or shop for groceries with Mom or Dad (no junk requests allowed).

Traffic may prevent younger students from walking or biking to school, but adults within reasonable distance have no excuse. Offer to accompany students who live in your neighborhood.

Make sure students have access to water throughout the day.

LAPS RUN THIS WEEK

PANDA TEAM

GRIZZLY TEAM

Talk about nutrition in terms of "body fuel," rather than "good" or "bad." Acknowledge that good taste matters. Encourage kids to choose what tastes good and helps their bodies perform.

Talk about exercise in terms of a "hunger to move." Let students know that their bodies are trying to tell them something when they feel restless and fidgety. Make "getting the wiggles out" a regular activity. Talk about how you feel afterward.

A year of healthy choices

Family Fit Lifestyle Month in **January** is a great opportunity for students to take home what they're learning at school. They can take a walk with a grandparent, prepare a healthy snack for a younger sibling, ride bikes with a cousin, or get good-for-you groceries with Mom or Dad.

Eating Disorders Awareness Week is during the last week of **February**. Have students share what they've learned about body image (in Chapter 5) with other classes.

Celebrate Barbie's birthday on **March** 9th, with a reality check. Compare Barbie's proportions to a real woman's (or take the measurements of a sporting teacher volunteer).

The fourth week in **April** is National TV Turnoff Week. Help students plan alternative activities for each evening.

May is Physical Fitness and Sports Month. Even less athletic students can have fun learning a new sport such as lawn bowling, gateball, or cricket. Wrap up the month with Good Stewardship Week.

June is National Fruit and Vegetable Month. It's also National Candy Month, but keep that to yourself.

July includes National Fried Chicken Day (6th), Video Games Day (8th), National Sugar Cookie Day (9th), National French Fries Day (13th), National Ice Cream Day (18th), and National Junk Food Day (21st). Celebrate in moderation.

October is National AIDS Awareness Month, and a great opportunity to focus on a health issue that affects millions of adults and children worldwide.

Get back on track in **August** with National Watermelon Day (3rd), Banana Lover's Day (27th) and National Trail Mix Day (31st).

In **November**, remind students to be thankful for "God's grocery store"—just like American Indians helped the pilgrims do at the first Thanksgiving.

National 5-a-Day Week is the second week in **September**. Visit www.dole5aday.com for more information.

Begin **December** with Eat an Apple Day (1st), and end it by helping students prepare for a Christmas that celebrates Jesus, not the toy and candy cane industries. Sponsor a child as a class, suggest that students donate their favorite toys to a shelter, or think of homemade or healthy gifts to exchange.

Organizations and resources

KidsHealth
The Nemours Foundation
1600 Rockland Road
Wilmington, DE 19803
(302) 651-4046
info@KidsHealth.org
www.kidshealth.org

Media Awareness Network
1500 Merivale Road, 3rd floor
Ottawa, ON
Canada
K2E 6Z5
613-224-7721
info@media-awareness.ca
www.media-awareness.ca

TV-Turnoff Network
1200 29th Street, NW
Lower Level #1
Washington, DC 20007
(202) 333-9220
email@tvturnoff.org
www.tvturnoff.org

Commercial Alert
4110 SE Hawthorne Blvd., #123
Portland, OR 97214
(503) 235-8012
ingo@commercialalert.org
www.commercialalert.org

Free The Children
233 Carlton Street
Thornhill, Ontario M5A 2L2
Canada
USA telephone: (800) 203-9091
www.freethechildren.com
info@freethechildren.com

World Health Organization
(American office)
525, 23rd Street, N.W.
Washington, DC 20037
(202) 974-3000
www.who.int
info@who.int

Recommended reading

Take Action! A Guide to Active Citizenship by Craig and Marc Kielburger: John Wiley & Sons, 2002. Step-by-step instructions for helping your students make a difference in the health of their hometown or the world.

Fast Food Nation: The Dark Side of the American Meal by Eric Schlosser: HarperCollins, 2002. A page-turner about a serious topic, this book is required reading for parents and teachers—and parts of it are accessible enough for an older student story time.

Fitness Fun by Emily Foster: Human Kinetics, 1992. Eighty-five games and activities to get students up and running.

Kids as Customers by James U. McNeal: Lexington Books, 1992. This and other books about marketing to children are eye opening. Parents, teachers, and students themselves deserve to know strategies used for "Kid Kustomers."

The Maker's Diet by Jordan S. Rubin N.M.D.,Ph.D. Siloam, 2004. Offers a natural health plan based on the Bible and tested by science.

Marty's Top Ten Diet and Fitness Strategies by Marty Copeland: Lion's Head Publishing, 2002. Offers keys to developing a healthy lifestyle by exercising the fruit of the Spirit and tips for incorporating fitness time into family time.

Chapter 1—It's my body! (Or is it?)

Do you not know that your body is a temple of the Holy Spirit, who is in you, whom you have received from God?
You are not your own; you were bought at a price. Therefore honor God with your body.
1 Corinthians 6:19-20

Understanding body stewardship starts with this simple question: why is it important to eat healthy foods and exercise? If we were honest, many of us would have to say it's because we want to look good. We also want to prevent diabetes and other diseases, and we know that being active and eating right makes us feel better, too. All of these answers are accurate, but from a Christian perspective, they're still incomplete. 1 Corinthians 6:19 teaches that our bodies—and the health and appearance of them—aren't really ours at all. As Christians, we have one reason for taking care of the Holy Spirit's temple: to honor God. Being fit is just icing on the cake (better make that peanut butter on apple slices).

Did you know?

"The earth is the LORD's, and everything in it, the world, and all who live in it." Psalm 24:1 is the key to understanding stewardship. Our bodies don't belong to us—not our head, feet, nose or toes. All of it is the Lord's.

Advertisers would like us to think that our bodies are worth only as much as they consume—from a 99-cent cheeseburger to a pair of $100 sneakers. What does 1 Corinthians 6:19-20 tell us the real value of our bodies is? Who bought our bodies and what price did He pay?

How do we treat another "temple"—our church building? Ask students to think about what would happen if we used the church as a garbage dump for our pizza crusts and half-empty soda cans. What are some examples of "junk" that we feed another temple—our body?

Selected Literature

A Quiet Place With Jesus: Meditation Themes for Kids by Anne Joan Flanagan: Pauline Books Media, 1996. (Devotional) 35 meditation, or contemplative prayer, themes for children.

The Healthy Body Cookbook by Joan D'Amico: John Wiley & Sons, 1999. Fifty-six healthy recipes arranged according to the parts of the body they benefit with complementary science activities.

Oh the Things You Can Do That Are Good for You!: All About Staying Healthy (Cat in the Hat's Learning Library) by Tish Rabe: Random House, 2001. (Picture book) A classic for all ages.

Choices

Ask students to think about the reasons they sometimes choose junk food and passive entertainment (TV, video games, internet) over healthier foods and activities. Start with questions like, "Why choose soda instead of water?" or "Why chat online instead of playing outside with your friends?" Write a few responses on the board: Discuss how honoring God should be the reason behind all of our decisions—not always how we feel or what we like.

Rise and shine!

Use this song to get students moving in the morning, or anytime the class needs an energy outlet. During the chorus, on *rise and shine*, students should stand tall and stretch their arms to the ceiling. At "drop and give me nine," have each student do whatever exercise they're comfortable with—nine somersaults, toe touches, sit-ups, pushups, etc. Got a whistle? Let students take turns having fun with the role of drill sergeant.

To the tune of "Rise and Shine"

Paul said to Corinth
Your body is a temple, temple.
Paul said to Corinth your body is a temple, temple.
It's really very simple, simple, simple.
Children of the Lord.

Rise and shine,
Then drop and give me nine.
Rise and shine,
Then drop and give me nine.
Rise and shine,
Don't let me hear you whine.
Children of the Lord.

Paul said to Corinth,
Honor God with your body, body.
Paul said to Corinth,
Honor God with your body, body.
Honor Him and get very sweaty, sweaty, sweaty.
Children of the Lord.

Holy Spirit on board

To understand how to treat our bodies with reverence, we can learn from expectant mothers. Is there a pregnant teacher, school staff member, or parent volunteer available to talk with the class? Have students ask her how she treats her body differently to protect the baby. She may avoid cigarette smoke in restaurants, or never drink wine with dinner. Maybe she has to be extra careful when exercising and doesn't lift heavy things.

After the discussion, tell students that we all have something precious inside our bodies that we need to be mindful of—not a baby, but the Holy Spirit! Explain that students' bodies don't need the same things that a pregnant woman needs, but they can be healthy in other ways. What do we know is good for children's bodies? Students may suggest sports, playing outside, limiting junk food, eating fruits and vegetables, getting enough sleep, and drinking water instead of soda.

This side up

Before class, find a special, delicate object, such as a glass ornament or a preserved butterfly. Write "Matthew 25:14-30" on a small piece of paper, then put the note and the object in a small box. Explain to students that your mystery package must be handled carefully, and students can take turns being responsible for it throughout the day. In the afternoon, lead students to a quiet location for a Bible study. Allow a volunteer to open the package and pass it around for the others to examine. Ask a student to look up the Bible reference and share it with the class.

Jesus' parable of the ten talents tells us that good stewards should work hard taking care of property that belongs to the person in charge. Discuss how our bodies are God's property, and have students suggest ways we can take care of them.

A silly grace has its place!

If I take part in the meal with thankfulness, why am I denounced because of something I thank God for?
So whether you eat or drink or whatever you do, do it all for the glory of God.
1 Corinthians 10:30-31

With pizza delivery, drive-up windows, and vending machines, it's easy to take food for granted. But giving thanks at mealtimes lets us acknowledge, on a regular basis, how dependent we are on God. Jesus is recorded "saying grace" nine times, and 1 Timothy 4:3 tells us that "God created [food] to be received with thanksgiving by those who believe and who know the truth." In 1 Corinthians 10:30-31, we learn that being thankful for what we eat is even more important that what we eat.

Before snack time and lunch, ask a student to lead the class in an original prayer. Or have the whole class recite one of these favorites:

Rubba-dub-dub,
Thanks for the grub.
Yay...God!
(unknown)

Lord,
Bless the food on our table.
Keep us healthy,
strong and able.
Margaret Kennedy

For every cup and plateful, Lord make us truly grateful.
(unknown)

Bless this bunch as they munch their lunch!
(unknown)

(To the tune of The Addams Family theme)

Da da da da (snap, snap) da da da da, (snap, snap) da da da da, da da da da, da da da da (snap, snap)
For this food we are so grateful.
We thank you for each plateful.
It always is so tasteful.
We thank you Lord our God.
Da da da da (snap, snap) Da da da da (snap, snap) Da da da da, da da da da, da da da da—Amen!
(unknown)

Mindless munching

Not only do we sometimes forget to say grace before eating, sometimes we forget we're eating at all. Ask for a show of hands—have students ever sipped on a soda while watching a movie, and before they know it, it's all gone? Who has ever been surprised to find they've finished off a bag of chips?

It's called mindless munching, and doctors say it's a major factor in childhood obesity. Help students develop good eating habits by setting aside some time everyday for snacking—and nothing else. Don't play videos or allow any schoolwork. Make it a social time, and encourage students to eat slowly.

Ask students to think about the taste of their food. Is it salty? Sweet? Sour? Bitter? Does some of the flavor go away if you hold your nose? What sound does the food make when you chew it? How does it feel in your mouth? Hot? Cold? Wet? Dry? Silky like milk or tingly like a pineapple?

Remind students to pay attention to their bodies' full feeling. Do some foods high in fiber or fat, such as nuts and vegetables; make you feel satisfied with less? How long after you're finished eating does it take to feel full?

Quiet time

Grown-ups have gardening, knitting, yoga and relaxation tapes, but quiet time is just as important to kids' health. Use Proverbs 17:22 as an example of the connection between physical health and spiritual health: "A cheerful heart is good medicine, but a crushed spirit dries up the bones." Studies show that meditation is a powerful medicine, reducing stress and even preventing heart disease!

Encourage students to set aside prayer time every day, before they're sleepy and in bed. Joshua 1:8 tells us to meditate on the law—students can use the time to read the Bible or a devotional, or just mull over one verse that puzzles them. If students keep a journal, they can write down their thoughts and questions. In Psalm 77:12 and 143:5, we see that David meditates on God's works. Allow students to find a place outdoors where they can reflect on creation— a critter, flower, or pattern in the clouds.

Be still and know . . .

Quieting exercises can improve concentration and relax students' minds before a test or other demanding event. Dim the lights (or light a candle in a dark room) and have each student find a spot to sit. White noise, such as a fan, may limit distractions. Soft sacred or classical music also sets a calm tone. Start with two or three minutes after lunch, and gradually increase to 10 or 15 minutes.

1. Ask students to sit still and upright, trying not to fidget, and close their eyes lightly.

2. Students should pay attention to their breathing, slowly inhaling through the nose and exhaling through the mouth.

3. Ask students to clear their minds of everyday clutter—tonight's homework or what's for lunch. The goal of meditation is to take our minds off ourselves and think about God.

4. Let each student choose a simple scripture or word to repeat under their breath, such as "Jesus" or "Jesus loves me." The Hebrew word that David used, hagah (daw gaw'), we translate "to meditate." The root meaning of the word is "whisper."

After a few meditations, have students complete the *Being Still* worksheet on page 16.

Name _____

Being Still

Read the passage of Scripture below and answer the questions.

The LORD said,
"Go out and stand on the mountain in the presence of the LORD, for the LORD is about to pass by."
Then a great and powerful wind tore the mountains apart and shattered the rocks before the LORD,
but the LORD was not in the wind. After the wind there was an earthquake, but the LORD was not in
the earthquake. After the earthquake came a fire, but the LORD was not in the fire. And after the
fire came a gentle whisper. When Elijah heard it, he pulled his cloak over his face and went out
and stood at the mouth of the cave. Then a voice said to him, "What are you doing
here, Elijah?"
1 Kings 19:11-13

1. How did God come to Elijah? _____
    A.   As an earthquake
    B.   In a powerful wind
    C.   As a gentle whisper
    D.   In a fire

2. Which way would you expect God to appear? Why?

    _____

3. Why do you think God chooses to speak quietly?

    _____

4. What noises could keep us from hearing God's voice?

    _____

5. Look up Psalm 46:10. How is being still one way to learn more about God?

    _____

6. Did you feel close to God or hear God's voice during meditation in class? _____

    Describe what you felt. Peaceful? Bored? Sleepy? Calm? Something else?

_____

The land of the fry

American children now get about 25% of their total "vegetable" servings in the form of French fries. With the new food guide pyramid (page 23), we can see that potatoes (especially fried ones) should be eaten sparingly and do not count as a vegetable serving. Help students get the vitamins and other nutrients they need from real vegetables by having a class French fry fast.

Start by discussing fasting with students. They may know Muslim families who fast from sunup to sundown during Ramadan, or they may have observed their own parents fasting. This type of fasting—going without any food for a certain period of time—should only be done by kids if their parents know about it and are helping them. (Fasting for weight loss can lead to eating disorders.) In another type of fasting, only one or two foods are given up, (for example, Lent in Orthodox Christianity).

Have students do this second type of fast as a class. Divide students into groups to compete to eat the fewest fries. Using the booklet on page 18, each student can record how many servings of fries he consumes in two weeks. Each day the class reaches their Zero goal, have a special treat—a favorite story, no homework night, or a snack of carrot or cucumber "chips" and julienne bell peppers "fries." Use the reproducible chart on page 19 to chart each group's progress.

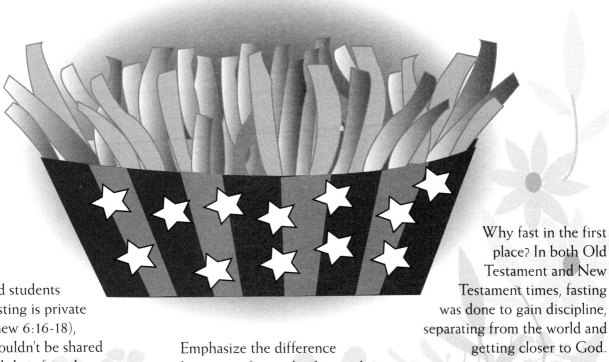

Remind students that fasting is private (Matthew 6:16-18), and shouldn't be shared with all their friends.

Emphasize the difference between a fast and a diet, and remind students that this is only a temporary fast—there are no "bad" or "sinful" foods. (1 Timothy 4:3-5)

Why fast in the first place? In both Old Testament and New Testament times, fasting was done to gain discipline, separating from the world and getting closer to God.

Dear Parent,

American children now get about one fourth of their total "vegetable" servings in the form of French fries. This high fat, low nutrition food should not take the place of real vegetables. As a class, we are reducing the amount of French fries and chips we consume through a French Fry Fast. Students will use this booklet to keep track of the number of times they eat French fries. Please encourage your child to choose carrots, spinach, cucumbers, squash, and other nutrient-packed veggies instead of fries. We hope students use the temptation to eat fries as a reminder to pray.

Thank you!

So whether you eat or drink or whatever you do, do it all for the glory of God.

1 Corinthians 10:31

Week Two

Monday _____
Tuesday _____
Wednesday _____
Thursday _____
Friday _____

Grand Total _____

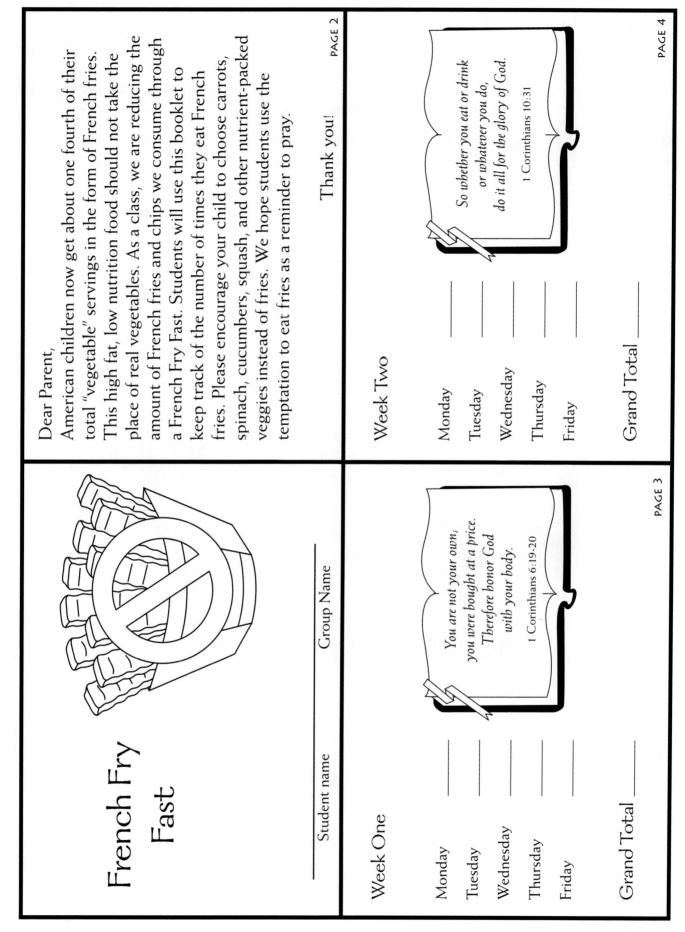

French Fry Fast

Student name _____

Group Name _____

You are not your own; you were bought at a price. Therefore honor God with your body.

1 Corinthians 6:19-20

Week One

Monday _____
Tuesday _____
Wednesday _____
Thursday _____
Friday _____

Grand Total _____

French fries and potato chips

Class Goal
ZERO

Week One

	(Group Name)	(Group Name)	(Group Name)
Monday			
Tuesday			
Wednesday			
Thursday			
Friday			
TOTAL			

Week Two

Monday			
Tuesday			
Wednesday			
Thursday			
Friday			
TOTAL			

Name_____

Learning to Honor

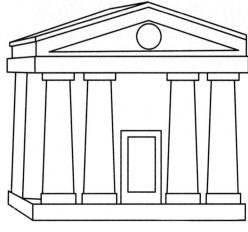

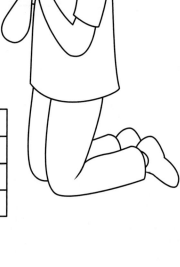

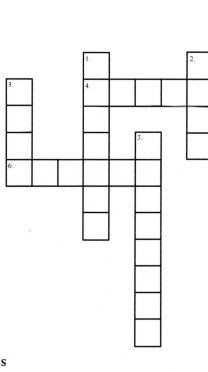

Across
4. to glorify, celebrate, praise, and respect
6. a sacred or holy building

Down
1. to speak softly
2. to communicate with God
3. to give up certain foods for a short time
5. to think about, also to whisper or muse

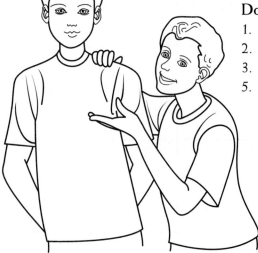

Chapter 2—Our daily bread

Give us today our daily bread.
Matthew 6:11

This part of the Lord's Prayer teaches us contentment as well as good nutrition. Students may be so accustomed to white bread, sweetened breakfast cereals, and other long-lasting convenience foods that the idea of "daily bread" is foreign.

Jesus taught over 2,000 years ago that we can trust God for the day-to-day provision of one of our most basic needs—bread. Today the U.S Department of Agriculture, in the food guide pyramid, advises us to eat whole grains—not refined grains—at most meals. Because whole grains have a shorter shelf life, they are indeed our daily bread. The following chapter will help students understand whole grains, a staple food in Bible times and the foundation of a healthy diet today.

Did you know?

Grains are packed with fiber and vitamins, but most breads and cereals are stripped of these nutrients to give them a lighter taste and longer shelf life. Read Isaiah 7:15 with students and talk about choosing the right foods.

Have students read about God providing manna to the Hebrew people in Exodus Chapter 16. What if, instead of trusting God for their "daily bread," they had figured out a way to make the manna last a long time by refining it and using preservatives?

In Psalm 41:9, David is betrayed by someone who shared his bread. Explain how sharing bread with someone was a symbol of friendship and intimacy. What do students share with their closest friends?

Winter Wheat by Brenda Z. Guiberson: Henry Holt & Company Inc., 1995. (Picture book) Let Stich the dog and Tulip the cow show students around the farm to learn about the planting and harvesting of wheat.

Rice Is Life by Rita Golden Gelman: Henry Holt & Company Inc., 2000. (Picture book) The life cycle of rice is described in beautifully illustrated poems and prose.

Corn Is Maize: The Gift of the Indians by Aliki: BT Bound, 1999. (Picture book) History and science combine to tell the magical story of corn.

The new food pyramid

The new food pyramid* (page 23) makes an important distinction between whole grains and "white," or refined, grains. White bread, white pasta, and white rice are no longer at the bottom of the pyramid with the "good" foods. Because they undergo a process that strips them of their nutritional value, these refined grains are now included at the top of the pyramid with sweets and saturated fats.

After sharing the food guide pyramids with students, take a moment before lunch and allow students to figure out how their meal fits into the new pyramid.

Discuss the strengths and weaknesses of students' lunches according the new pyramid. Have students think of ways their lunches could be made healthier.

What foods would students need at other meals and snack times to complete the pyramid? (For example, because this lunch does not include any nuts or legumes, students could snack on almonds or sunflower seeds, and have a bean burrito or chili for dinner).

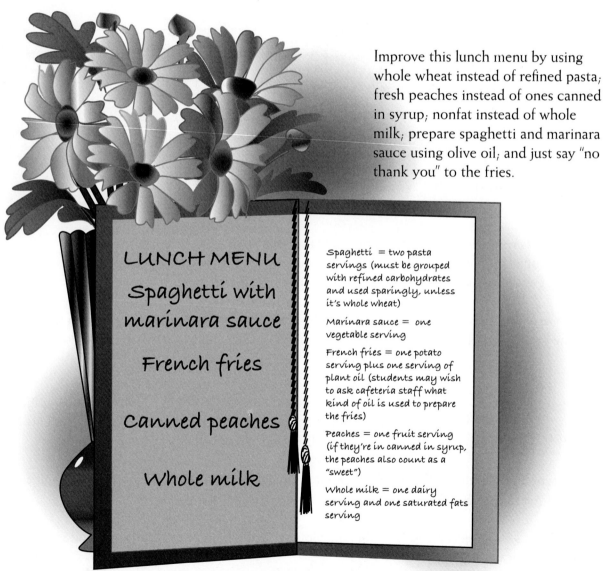

Improve this lunch menu by using whole wheat instead of refined pasta; fresh peaches instead of ones canned in syrup; nonfat instead of whole milk; prepare spaghetti and marinara sauce using olive oil; and just say "no thank you" to the fries.

LUNCH MENU

Spaghetti with marinara sauce

French fries

Canned peaches

Whole milk

Spaghetti = two pasta servings (must be grouped with refined carbohydrates and used sparingly, unless it's whole wheat)

Marinara sauce = one vegetable serving

French fries = one potato serving plus one serving of plant oil (students may wish to ask cafeteria staff what kind of oil is used to prepare the fries)

Peaches = one fruit serving (if they're in canned in syrup, the peaches also count as a "sweet")

Whole milk = one dairy serving and one saturated fats serving

* The new food pyramid was scheduled to be released by the USDA shortly after this book was printed. The model on page 23 is based on projections made by *Scientific American*, January 2003.

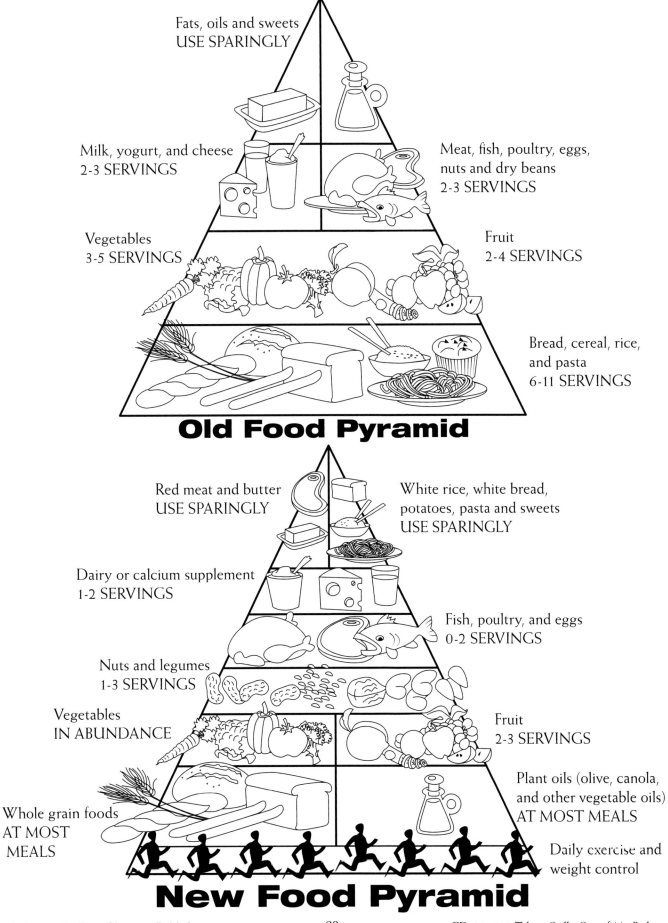

Fats, oils and sweets
USE SPARINGLY

Milk, yogurt, and cheese
2-3 SERVINGS

Meat, fish, poultry, eggs,
nuts and dry beans
2-3 SERVINGS

Vegetables
3-5 SERVINGS

Fruit
2-4 SERVINGS

Bread, cereal, rice,
and pasta
6-11 SERVINGS

Old Food Pyramid

Red meat and butter
USE SPARINGLY

White rice, white bread,
potatoes, pasta and sweets
USE SPARINGLY

Dairy or calcium supplement
1-2 SERVINGS

Fish, poultry, and eggs
0-2 SERVINGS

Nuts and legumes
1-3 SERVINGS

Vegetables
IN ABUNDANCE

Fruit
2-3 SERVINGS

Whole grain foods
AT MOST
MEALS

Plant oils (olive, canola,
and other vegetable oils)
AT MOST MEALS

Daily exercise and
weight control

New Food Pyramid

Did they get it right this time?

There is a way that seems right to a man, but in the end it leads to death.
Proverbs 14:12

*Whatever is good and perfect comes to us from God above, who created all heaven's lights …
He never changes or casts shifting shadows.*
James 1:17, NLT

Use the food pyramid charts on page 23 and discuss the changes that were made. Point out how white rice, white bread, potatoes, and pasta went from the bottom of the pyramid (with the good foods) to the top (foods to use sparingly). With such flip-flopping advice, students may wonder what information they can really trust. We can look to God's revelation, both in the Bible and in creation, to guide our eating choices.

God's grocery store

One of God's revelations about how to eat can be found in creation—God's grocery store. We should eat stuff that God created for food, before it's changed into something people think might be better. Go through the following list with students and decide if the items were made by God—or people— for food.

White sandwich bread
Sunflower seeds
Apples
Breakfast cereal with artificial apple flavor
Water
Cola
Honey
Candy bar
Granola bar

Food in the Bible

Another way we can learn how to eat is by paying attention to what food God provides people in the Bible. Have students look up Deuteronomy 8:7-8. God gives His people a "good land" full of wheat, barley, and olive oil. Jesus created fish and bread to feed the multitude—these foods must be good for us, too. Have students research other Bible foods, using a Bible dictionary, concordance, or Bible customs and manners reference book.

Breaking bread

Laughter and bread go together.
Ecclesiastes 10:19 THE MESSAGE

Drive-thru fast food windows, meal replacement bars, and TV dinners…eating this way may be efficient, but is it healthy? Is it Christian? Share Acts 2:42,46 with students:

[Early Christians] devoted themselves to the apostles' teaching and to the fellowship, to the breaking of bread and to prayer…
They broke bread in their homes and ate together with glad and sincere hearts.
Acts 2:42,46

Explain to students that "breaking of bread" isn't just referring to communion—it also means eating a meal. God didn't intend for us to wolf down our food on the way to do something more important. Have students think of instances of Jesus using meals to teach and build relationships. For example, the breakfast by the sea (John 21), Jesus' miracle at the wedding banquet (John 2), the feast at Levi's house (Luke 5), and the Passover meal (Mark 14). When we eat, what is our main goal?

Do students agree that eating with friends makes their hearts "glad"? We know today that when we enjoy a meal with others, we tend to eat more slowly and avoid overeating. If you have any leeway available, allow your class extra time for lunch. Encourage students to focus on fellowship by holding hands to give thanks, and putting God and their classmates first.

The good news

Grains are a wonderful blessing. They provide many of the vitamins, minerals, and other nutrients we need, and are grown all over the world. Different types of grain—wheat, corn, rice, oats, barley—all have the same basic composition.

Recreate or copy the diagram below for students and explain the different parts of the wheat kernel. Then, have students complete the worksheet on the following page.

Wheat Kernel Diagram

Bran—The layered outer covering of the kernel contains most of the nutrients, including minerals and fiber. Bran is stripped away in most refined products like white bread and pasta.

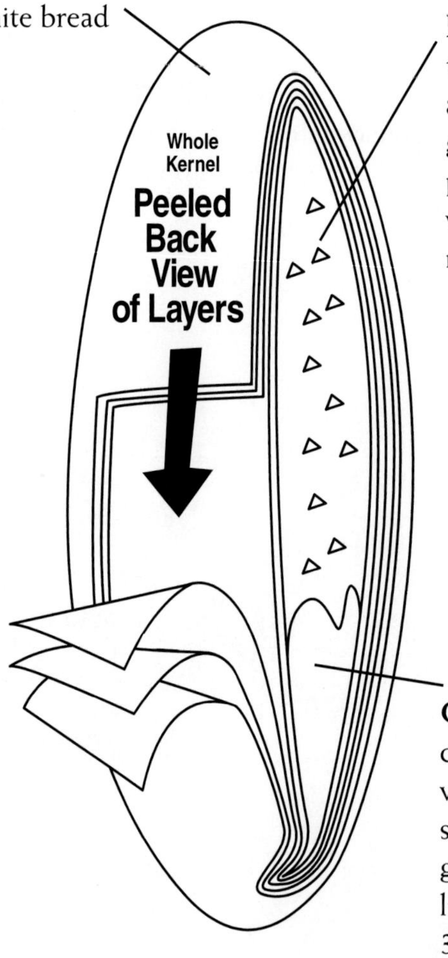

Whole Kernel

Peeled Back View of Layers

Endosperm—The heaviest part of the grain, the endosperm contains most of the protein and carbohydrates. The protein found in grain is healthier and of higher quality than protein from meat, and becomes "complete" when you eat it with vegetables, beans, or nuts.

Germ—The smallest part of the grain, germ contains polyunsaturated fats. These fats are very healthy, but are removed during milling so that the flour has a longer shelf-life. The germ is rich in vitamins E and B, and shaped like a kidney or a bean. In Deuteronomy 32:14 KJV, Moses sings about God giving man "the fat of kidneys of wheat" for food!

Some grains, like rice or oats, are covered by a papery sheath called the hull or chaff. It protects the nutrients inside and has to be removed before the grain can be eaten or processed.

Name_____

Wheat Kernel Worksheet

Grains are members of the grass family. We only eat the seed, or kernel. Label the different parts of the wheat kernel.

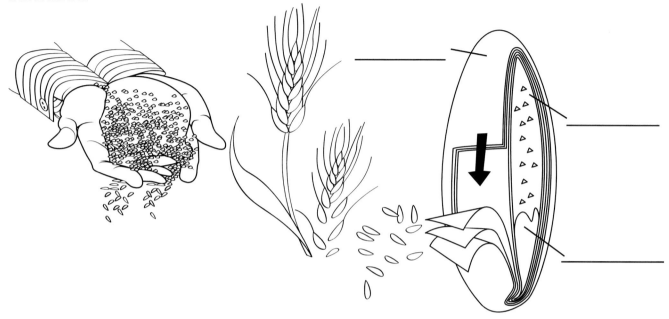

1. White flour is made using only the endosperm part of the kernel. What kind of flour uses the whole kernel?

   _____

2. "On a certain sabbath Jesus was walking through a field of ripe grain. His disciples were pulling off heads of grain, rubbing them in their hands to get rid of the chaff, and eating them." (Luke 6:1, THE MESSAGE) What part of the grain are the disciples eating?

   _____

3. What nutrients do they get from eating the entire grain?

   _____

4. What does God say about picking heads of grain from someone else's field in Deuteronomy 23:25?

   _____

   _____

The bad news

Materials

    Wheat, corn kernels, or other seeds from grain
    Stones for grinding or mortar and pestle
    Sieve
    White bread
    Whole wheat bread

Flour is simple enough to make—for thousands of years people have been grinding seeds into powder. Take students outside to experiment with grinding flour by hand.

1. If necessary, have students remove the hull, or chaff, by hand.

2. When students have produced some powdery flour, have them sift it though a sieve, then continue grinding the larger pieces.

3. Talk about how this process uses the entire seed—bran, endosperm, and germ. (In most mills today, only the endosperm is used).

Afterward, compare the students' grinding process to modern mills using the following description of the modern milling process:

> High speed "hammers" move very fast to crush the grain. The heat kills many nutrients, including live enzymes and vitamins. Bran and germ, the most healthy parts of the grain, are sifted out. Artificial preservatives must be added to increase shelf life. The flour may be exposed to chemicals—chlorine gas or benzoyl peroxide—to bleach it white. Synthetic thiamin, riboflavin, niacin, and iron must be added, and the flour or bread is labeled "enriched." A perfect example of people changing God's food into something they think is better! Have students look at the ingredients on the package of white bread to see these additives.

Plan a field trip to a nearby flour mill for first-hand experience.

According to a National Food Consumption Survey, children aren't getting the dietary fiber they need. The American Health Foundation recommends that children add 5 to their age to determine how many grams of fiber they should eat. For example, a peanut butter and raspberry jam sandwich on whole wheat bread, with a pear for dessert, meets the daily fiber needs (13 grams) of a seven-year old. Eating from God's grocery store—whole grains, fruits, vegetables, nuts, and beans—automatically provides children with plenty of dietary fiber which helps children feel full longer, and thus helps prevent overeating. Eating enough fiber also prevents diabetes, heart disease, and some types of cancer.

Animal intelligence

*Even the stork in the sky knows her appointed seasons, and the dove, the swift and the thrush
observe the time of their migration. But my people do not know the requirements of the LORD.*
Jeremiah 8:7

*But ask the animals, and they will teach you, or the birds of the air, and they will tell you;
or speak to the earth, and it will teach you, or let the fish of the sea inform you.*
Job 12:7-8

We like to pride ourselves on what separates us from the animals. Jesus tells us that we could benefit from being more like animals. (Remember "the birds of the air" and "the lilies of the field" in Matthew Chapter 6). Animals can also teach us about health and nutrition, as students can observe in the following demonstration:

Materials
    Whole wheat flour
    White flour
    Fish tank
    Meal worms (available at most pet stores)

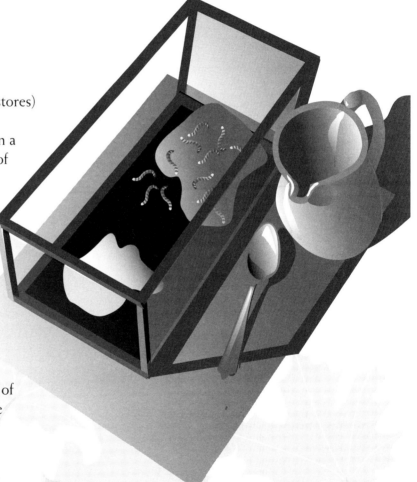

1. Take an empty fish tank outside—in a covered area—and put a cup each of white and wheat flour on opposite sides.

2. Create labels for each side that read "white" and "whole wheat," or use white and whole wheat bread packaging to help students visualize the associate between the type of flour (white or whole wheat) and the type of bread.

3. Place the meal worms in the center of the tank, and have students observe which flour they are attracted to.

Discussion
With what they've learned about the milling process, do students understand why animals may avoid white bread?

Breakfast: the most important meal of the day. But it could possibly be better to skip it than to eat what some of us tend to: sweetened cereals, pre-packaged breakfast bars, and toaster pastries. Have students bring in empty boxes of these items, along with cookie boxes, candy bar wrappers, and other sweets. Read the ingredients and nutritional data, and compare these types of breakfast foods to the dessert foods. Copy and cut out the sheet below for students to record their results. Are children surprised at how much the breakfast foods have in common with sweets?

Name _____

Magically Deceptive

Breakfast food:_____

First three ingredients:

_____

_____

_____

Bad for you

Sugars (g): _____

Saturated fat (g): _____

Good for you

Fiber (g): _____

Protein (g): _____

Does it contain artificial flavors? _____

Does it contain artificial colors? _____

Candy:_____

First three ingredients:

_____

_____

_____

Bad for you

Sugars (g): _____

Saturated fat (g): _____

Good for you

Fiber (g): _____

Protein (g): _____

Does it contain artificial flavors? _____

Does it contain artificial colors? _____

Corn syrup puffs

How's a kid supposed to know which breakfast foods are good for them and which are full of corn syrup and hydrogenated oils? The ingredient list on most cereals is hidden away, lost among all the bright colors, games, and fun characters.

Let students create their own, more honest products. They can come up with their own product names and create packaging designs for common breakfast items. Ask students to think about if the product is really as healthy as the box would have them believe. What are the health effects of eating too much sugar—does it make you happy and healthy like the TV commercials show? Encourage students to consider the ingredients—does the product contain cocoa, fruit, apples, or charms? What does it contain instead? Where and how is the product made—in a rainforest by toucans, or in a factory?

If students feel the box is misleading, how do they think it should be represented? Allow them to create their own designs, and then glue them to a empty cereal boxes. Talk about how the new names and illustrations change how students feel about the product.

Train your senses

Cannot my taste discern perverse things? Job 6:30 KJV

Researchers agree that snacking is an important way for children to get the energy and nutrients they need between meals. But studies have shown that processed, sugar-filled snacks are contributing to obesity, diabetes, and other health problems in children. Help students establish healthy snacking habits with the following exercise:

Begin with a discussion of students' favorite snacks. What do most students prefer—fruits, veggies, and nuts, or packaged sweets? Which come from God's grocery store, and which are man-made?
Do students think that the healthy snacks don't taste as good? Explain that we all tend to prefer the taste of whatever foods we're used to. Making the switch from sweetened, refined foods to whole foods takes practice. Share Hebrews 5:14 with students:

> *But solid food is for the mature, who because of practice have their senses trained to discern good and evil.*
> Hebrews 5:14 NASB

Snack booklet

Explain to students that taste is one of our five senses, and we can train it to tell the difference between healthy foods and unhealthy foods. Challenge students to "train their senses" by eating healthy snacks for one week. Reproduce the snack booklet on pages 33-34 for each student.

Surprise students occasionally with a snack time spelling bee—quiz each student on the spelling the ingredients of whatever snack they brought from home or purchased at school. Students who chose an apple can breathe a collective sigh of relief, but woe to the student who selected anything containing high fructose corn syrup, partially hydrogenated soybean oil, or xanthan gum!

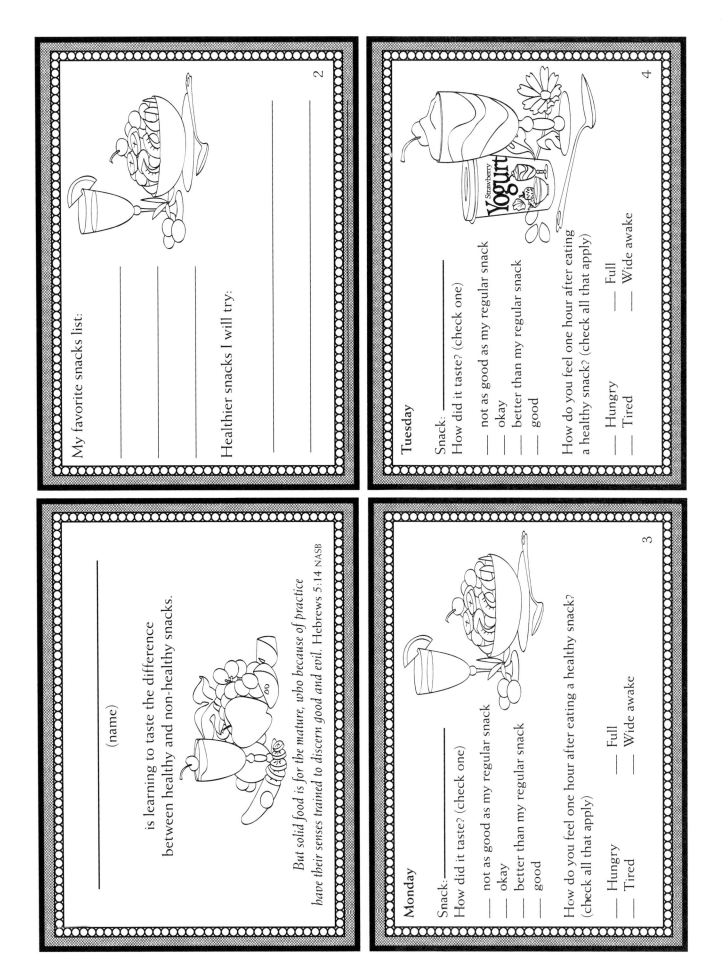

Card 2

My favorite snacks list:

_____

Healthier snacks I will try:

_____

2

Card 4

Tuesday

Snack: _____

How did it taste? (check one)

___ not as good as my regular snack
___ okay
___ better than my regular snack
___ good

How do you feel one hour after eating
a healthy snack? (check all that apply)

___ Hungry   ___ Full
___ Tired   ___ Wide awake

4

Card 1

_____
(name)

is learning to taste the difference
between healthy and non-healthy snacks.

*But solid food is for the mature, who because of practice
have their senses trained to discern good and evil.* Hebrews 5:14 NASB

Card 3

Monday

Snack: _____

How did it taste? (check one)

___ not as good as my regular snack
___ okay
___ better than my regular snack
___ good

How do you feel one hour after eating a healthy snack?
(check all that apply)

___ Hungry   ___ Full
___ Tired   ___ Wide awake

3

CD-204008 *Taking Godly Care of My Body*

Wednesday

5

Snack: _____

How did it taste? (check one)
— not as good as my regular snack
— okay
— better than my regular snack
— good

How do you feel one hour after eating a healthy snack?
(check all that apply)

— Hungry   — Full
— Tired   — Wide awake

Thursday

6

Snack: _____

How did it taste? (check one)
— not as good as my regular snack
— okay
— better than my regular snack
— good

How do you feel one hour after eating a healthy snack?
(check all that apply)

— Hungry   — Full
— Tired   — Wide awake

Friday

7

Snack: _____

How did it taste? (check one)
— not as good as my regular snack
— okay
— better than my regular snack
— good

How do you feel one hour after eating
a healthy snack? (check all that apply)

— Hungry   — Full
— Tired   — Wide awake

8

What new, healthy snacks do you like now?

_____
_____
_____
_____

Make everyday healthy snack day!

Make healthy-snack time fun by reading students' favorite stories or going outside for a picnic.

Assign students a healthy snack to bring in once a month for the entire class.

To encourage students to try new healthy foods, have days when each student can share part of her snack with another student.

Keep a list of healthy snacks posted in the classroom. When a student brings in a new food, help the others determine if it can be added to the list.

POWER SNACKS FOR
MR. JORDAN'S CLASS

MINI-SANDWICHES ON WHOLE WHEAT

MULTI-GRAIN BREAD WITH PEANUT BUTTER OR CHEESE

FRUIT (APPLES, BLUEBERRIES, ORANGES, BANANAS, PEARS)

NUTS AND SEEDS (ALMONDS, SUNFLOWER SEEDS, WALNUTS)

VEGETABLES (BABY CARROTS, BROCCOLI, BELL PEPPERS, SPINACH)

YOGURT WITH FRUIT OR FOR DIPPING VEGGIES

CHEESE OR COTTAGE CHEESE WITH WHOLE WHEAT CRACKERS

BEVERAGES: WATER, MILK, OR FRUIT JUICE

Name _____

Whole Grain Word Search

cereal
breakfast cereal
hull
germ
bran
endosperm
flour
whole wheat bread
white bread
refined flour
breaking bread
fiber
enriched

```
Y E H H C M V L W O I G B D M E B W
E W P B A F I B E R K O O S X E R E
Z B H B O O C H K J G E A I B C E G
D R C O N C V C X N R K D L D S A S
Q E E I L F W H I T E B R E A D K Z
M A R Z Q E N R I C H E D P Y Y I A
W K E R O I W L E E S Y A M K U N N
F F A Q E X D H B I F B Q Q K L G U
Q A L E Z F G Z E Z A U R F D Z B E
M S B W T F I E I A K J D A B Z R E
C T I H V T M N R K T C D O N Y E N
D C V U Q R X V E M C B Q L H I A D
G E P L T I P V U D P J R M S R D O
D R Q L F E Z I M F F O O E L M R S
I E F N H X A N E Y L L R B A U N P
P A Y O K C Q R V J F O O V S D I E
E L I Y N F W V A X K P U U E W P R
Y O N E N O V W I J I X D R R L B M
C G L O B L V U S Q G O A J L Y X Q
```

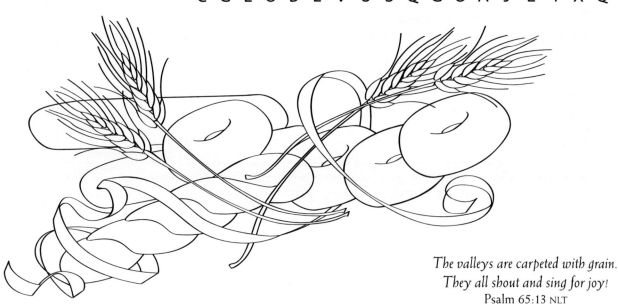

Chapter 3—All your strength

Love the Lord your God with all your heart and with all your soul and with all your mind and with all your strength.
Mark 12:30

A Christian education helps children learn how to love God with their hearts, souls, and minds. What about strength? It's not just for bulging body builders! The classroom and school grounds offer lots of opportunities for students to be physically active.

Fitness prevents disease and helps self-esteem, but Mark 12:30 tells us more: being strong is part of the greatest commandment! The following games and activities will get students moving—helping them grow strong (literally!) in the Lord.

Did you know?

In Genesis 3:19, God tells Adam "by the sweat of your brow you will eat your food." Our bodies aren't designed to sit in a chair all day, five days a week. Use it, don't lose it!

In Psalm 150:4, we learn to "Praise him with tambourine and dancing." Men and women throughout history have recognized the spiritual value of dance, including Aaron's sister Miriam (Exodus 15:20) and King David! Dancing is also great for our bodies—improving strength, balance, and cardiovascular health.

2 Samuel 6:14 tells us that "David...danced before the Lord with all his might." Ask students to think about this alternative: "David hobbled around for awhile but was so out of shape he got tired really fast and collapsed on the sofa."

Selected Literature

Work Out: Active Devotions for Teens by Steve Wunderink: CRC Publications, 2000. (Devotional)

Children's Book of Yoga: Games & Exercises That Mimic Plants & Animals & Objects by Thia Luby: Clear Light Publications, 1999. (Non-fiction) Make exercise fun and imaginative by allowing students to mimic the positions and shapes in nature.

Shake-It-Up Tales!: Stories to Sing, Dance, Drum, and Act Out by Margaret Read MacDonald: August House Publications, 1999. This book helps make story time active.

I Hope You Dance (Children's Book) by Mark D. Sanders: Rutledge Hill Press, 2003 (Picture book) Whimsical take on the adult best-seller.

Jumping jacks

Get students' feet jumping and their hearts pumping with this memory verse game:

Two students turn the rope and chant (substituting the jumper's name for Jack):

> *Jack, be nimble.*
> *Jack, be quick.*
> *Jump right in*
> *And say your pick.*

The jumper hops in and recites a Bible verse while jumping. (Students may choose a verse from the Scripture Index on pages 78-79).

BMP

Complement physical activities with a small math lesson by having students measure their heart rates. Compare rates during exercise to a resting heart rate taken after a quiet meditation time. Have students practice finding the pulse in their wrists or necks, using the index and middle finger. Have them count the number of pulses in a 15 second period. Multiply the number by 4 to find beats per minute (BMP).

Students can find their maximum heart rate by subtracting their age from 220. For example, the maximum heart rate for a ten year old is 210. Because we're supposed to exercise at 70 to 90% of our maximum heart rate, the same ten year old could exercise safely between 147 and 189 beats per minute. Advanced students can calculate their exercise zones.

Shake what God gave you

Tambourines and other rattling instruments are a fun (and Biblical) complement to praise dancing. And they're simple to make:

Tambourines

Materials

       Paper plates or disposable pie pans

       Bells, small stone, or other items that will rattle

       Crayons, markers, paint, sponges

       Stapler or tape

       Ribbons, crepe paper, or streamers

Give each student two paper plates, or pie pans, and crayons or markers. Have them decorate the bottom of each plate. Suggest Bible verses such as 2 Samuel 6:14, Psalm 30:11, Psalm 150, and Exodus 15:20 for students to look up and incorporate into their designs if they wish. Next put small bells, stones or other objects in one plate. Place the other plate face down on top of the first. Tape or staple the plates together. Attach ribbons, crepe paper, or streamers.

Shakers

Materials

       Rice or seeds

       Boxes, bottles, clean aluminum cans, or other small, empty containers

       Crayons, markers, paint, sponges, scraps of fabric and glue

Have students decorate containers and then fill with rice or seeds.

When the instruments have dried, put on a praise tape and encourage students to move to the music and experiment with rhythm.

Jump for joy!

Dance is part of worship in both the Old and New Testaments, but its importance has been diminished in English translations. For instance, the word agalliao (ag-al-lee-ah'-o) is derived from a root verb that means to jump for joy. It appears many times in the New Testament, but it's translated "to rejoice" or "be glad."

Look up the following verses and have students substitute "spring up like gushing water," "leap," or "jump for joy" instead of the boldface words. Discuss the difference between the traditional translations and students' new ones—which better conveys the excitement of Jesus and His followers?

[Jesus] **rejoiced greatly** in the Holy Spirit. Luke 10:21 NASB

The jailer brought them into his house and set a meal before them; he was **filled with joy** because he had come to believe in God—he and his whole family. Acts 16:34

Rejoice and be **glad**, because great is your reward in heaven.
Matthew 5:12

Therefore my heart is **glad** and
my tongue rejoices;
my body also will live
in hope.
Acts 2:26

Get your godly groove on

Freestyle dancing can be intimidating at first for shy students. Get everyone moving with these simple, choreographed moves:

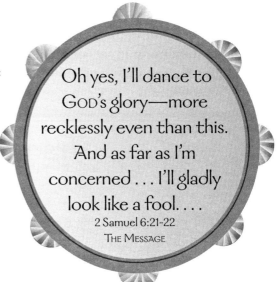

Oh yes, I'll dance to
GOD's glory—more
recklessly even than this.
And as far as I'm
concerned . . . I'll gladly
look like a fool. . . .
2 Samuel 6:21-22
THE MESSAGE

To the tune of *Skip to My Lou*

Praise, praise, praise Him with dancing,
Praise, praise, praise Him with dancing,
Praise, praise, praise Him with dancing,
Praise Him with dancing, my children.

Love him with all your strength, strength, strength,
Love him with all your strength, strength, strength,
Love him with all your strength, strength, strength,
Love Him with dancing, my children.

1. Stand in a circle and clap hands (as you sing the chorus).
2. Hold hands and walk into the circle, raising joined hands as you meet in the center; back out to your original position, lowering hands (as you sing the verses). Repeat.

Dancing in front of peers is sometimes just as hard for self-conscious children as it is for adults. Encourage students with David's words in 2 Samuel 6:21-22 (above).

Do you know Jehovah Chezeq?

Let them praise his name with dancing. . . . Psalm 149:3

The names of God in the Bible help us understand different aspects of His nature. Jehovah Chezeq (yeh-ho-vah' khay'-zek), from Psalm 18:1 KJV, literally means "Lord of my strength!"

To the tune of *Do you know the Muffin Man?*

Oh, do you know Jehovah Chezeq?
Jehovah Chezeq?
Jehovah Chezeq?
Oh, do you know Jehovah Chezeq?
The Lord of my strength.
Oh, yes I know Jehovah Chezeq,
Jehovah Chezeq,
Jehovah Chezeq,
Oh, yes I know Jehovah Chezeq,
The Lord of my strength.

Students hold hands and skip in a circle. On "Lord of my strength," students stop and flex their biceps or strike another "strong" pose.

The Lord will watch over your coming and going

By walking or biking to school, students can be great stewards of the environment and their bodies. Have students poll other classes to learn how many students already get to and from school on their own two feet (or two wheels).

Transportation Survey

Teacher: _____

Grade: _____

Number of students: _____

Number of students who walk or bike: _____

Tally the reasons other students don't walk or bike:

    Live too far away

    Traffic

    Just don't want to

    No bike racks

    Would take too long

Have students think of ways more students would be able to walk or bike to school. For example:

- Have a crossing guard at certain intersections

- Install bike racks

- Plan safe trails to nearby neighborhoods

- Ask parents to lead walking and biking groups

 CD-204008 *Taking Godly Care of My Body*

The Earth will teach you

"But ask the animals, and they will teach you, or the birds of the air, and they will tell you;
or speak to the earth, and it will teach you, or let the fish of the sea inform you."
Job 12:7-8

Working outside in a garden nurtures students' appreciation of creation, offers many hands-on learning opportunities, and it's great exercise! Start with a traditional vegetable or flower garden, or choose a fun theme:

Habitat garden
Design a home for wildlife from a simple clay pot and saucer, or place large rocks in direct sunlight for a lizard lounge.

Vegetable garden
Even picky eaters have a hard time resisting veggies grown by their own hands. Include a couple foods students might not try otherwise, such as squashes, beets, peas, or Brussels sprouts.

Bible garden
With everything from grapevines to reeds and bulrushes, students can experience sights, tastes, and smells from the Bible first-hand.

Pizza garden
Students can create a pie-shaped garden divided into "slices" of tomatoes, oregano, basil, and onions. Buon appetito!

Gardening Tips
Keep the garden a manageable and enjoyable size. Work with small plants instead of seeds to see quicker results.

Even a small garden takes a lot of work. Enlist parent volunteers on planting day.

Choose a spot close to your classroom that has good soil and receives the right amount of sunlight.

Remember to use absolutely no chemicals in a children's garden. Create a compost bin and pick off bugs by hand. Plant beneficial herbs, marigolds, onions, and garlic to help keep bugs away.

Biblical Dancing

ACROSS:
3. a jump for joy
4. being strong

DOWN:
1. a name for God that means "God of my strength"
2. to move to music, or to jump or skip

1. In 2 Samuel 6:21-22, what does David do for the Lord that makes him look "like a fool?"

_____

2. "Love the Lord your God with all your heart and with all your soul and with all your mind and with

all your _____ ." Mark 12:30

Chapter 4—Created in Whose image?

I praise you because I am fearfully and wonderfully made. . . .
Psalm 139:14

When David sang these words, he wasn't comparing himself to an airbrushed cover model, or thinking *if only my abs were a little more chiseled.* He doesn't grumble about the way his ears stick out, or worry about being too tall or too short. He simply worships the awesome Designer who created his wonderful body—wonderful despite its freckles, crooked teeth, or skinny legs.

Negative body image, for the most part, used to be an issue for teenage girls. Now young children of both sexes are affected by the media's constant parade of hard bodies. The first defense is helping students understand in Whose image they were created—now that's positive body image!

Did you know?

Even kids who don't watch a lot of TV are still overexposed to the world's definition of beauty—billboards on the highway, in-store music lyrics—even magazine covers in the check-out aisle. Encourage students to be aware of these messages, and remember to guard their hearts (Proverbs 4:23) at all times.

Studies have shown that almost half of first-, second- and third-grade girls want to be thinner, and 40% fourth-graders say they diet very often or sometimes. It only gets worse as students get older— 81% of ten-year-olds admit to dieting or binge eating, according to the Harvard Eating Disorders Clinic. One five-year-old was found to be eating paper to fill herself up, and running circles around her room at night to burn calories.

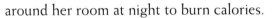

Selected Literature

Food Fight: A Guide to Eating Disorders for Preteens and Their Parents by Janet Bode: Aladdin Library, 1998. Discusses how eating disorders begin in childhood and helps preteens, teachers, and parents learn to break harmful patterns.

Food Rules: The Stuff You Munch, Its Crunch, Its Punch, and Why You Sometimes Lose Your Lunch by Bill Haduch: Dutton Books, 2001. Combines humor and science to teach food, nutrition and digestion. Promotes healthy body image by focusing on the amazing things our bodies do, not just what they look like.

Games for Actors and Non-Actors by Augusto Boal: Routledge, 2002. Drama is a fun, active, and effective way to help students deal with any important issue they face, including body image. Kids especially love Boal's Forum Theater (akin to the role-playing exercises in this chapter) and Invisible Theater!

Emotional eating

Some children cope with their lonely, nervous, sad, and stressed out feelings by eating—a very dangerous habit. Because the child's needs are temporarily "fixed" with food, depression and anxiety can go untreated well into adulthood. Encourage students to always make sure they're eating because they're hungry, not because they're disappointed or afraid or anything else. Share Exodus 20:3 with students Don't let any food become your God. Go over different feelings with students and have them brainstorm ways to deal with problems without using food.

Disordered eating

Eating disorders are rare, but children as young as 5 or 6 are developing poor body-esteem that can lead to anorexia nervosa, compulsive overeating, and bulimia nervosa. These complex disorders are not caused by the media or any other single factor, but are often connected to anxiety, depression, or abuse. The following behavior may indicate an eating disorder (even if the students appears to be a normal weight), and counseling is necessary:

- Wearing baggy clothes or dressing in layers to hide body shape or weight loss

- Frequent trips to the bathroom immediately following meals (sometimes running water to hide the sound of vomiting)

- Shifting the food around on the plate, cutting food into tiny pieces

- Hiding food in strange places to avoid eating or to eat at a later time

- Flushing uneaten food down the toilet (can cause sewage problems)

- Low self-esteem, complaining of being "stupid" or "fat," especially after eating

When I'm feeling Sad,
1. I ask God to comfort me,
2. Cry.
3. Hug somebody.
When I'm feeling guilty,
I ask for forgiveness!
When I'm feeling stressed,
I have my quiet time.
When I'm feeling loney,
1. I ask mom or Dad for some one on one time.
2. Call Grandma.
3. E-mail my pen pal.

Thumbody special

Materials
   Paper
   Stamp pads
   Mirrors
   Soap and water for washing up

The world may want us to all wear the same clothes and eat the same cheeseburger, but God loves His diverse creation! No two of us are alike, just as no two thumbprints are alike. Have students create self-portraits using only their thumbprints. Encourage them to look in the mirror closely and not just guess or assume what they look like. In pencil, students may write their names in the lower right-hand corner. Let dry and display for students to study. Can students see how each thumbprint is different? How are faces just as unique as thumbprints?

Body image survey

Ask students to think about their own body image. Do they see their bodies as healthy? How do they think others perceive their bodies? Allow students to complete the anonymous survey on page 48. Remind students not to put their names on the worksheet. Discuss the collective results as a class.

Body Image Survey

Circle the most appropriate answer and write out your answer to question number 3.

Sex: male or female

1. Do you weigh yourself often, at least once a week and sometimes more than once a day?

    Yes or No

I praise you, because I am fearfully and wonderfully made. -Psalm 139:14

2. Do you wish you could change your body?

    Yes or No

3. If yes, what would you change?

    _____

4. Do you exercise mainly to lose weight?

    Yes or No

5. Do you worry about how thin or muscular you are?

    Yes or No

6. Do you compare your body to people on TV?

    Yes or No

7. Have you avoided situations where people could see your body, for example, sports, swimming pools, the beach, etc.?

    Yes or No

If you answered yes to many of these questions, you may be trying to obtain an unrealistic body type. We can base how we feel about our bodies on God's word, not what adults or friends think, or what we see on television. Always remember that you are "fearfully and wonderfully made" (Psalm 139:14).

Outward appearance

Ask students to discuss prejudices that exist against people who are overweight. View TV, commercial, or magazine clips in class and note how rarely overweight (or even average-sized) characters appear. Actors of different sizes are becoming more common, but most leading men and women are thinner than average.

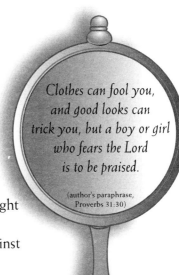

Clothes can fool you, and good looks can trick you, but a boy or girl who fears the Lord is to be praised.

(author's paraphrase, Proverbs 31:30)

Choose two or three clips that do include overweight characters, and discuss whether or not the people are portrayed fairly. Typically, an overweight character is shown as lazy, the bad guy, or the one with no friends. Remind students that these jokes or stereotypes are just as harmful as prejudices against minorities, women, or other groups. Go over the quiz below to identify and correct size prejudice.

True or false?

1. Overweight people eat more than thinner people.
    False: For the most part, the shape of our bodies is genetic and we can only change it slightly by what we eat. Some people are naturally bigger, even if they eat the same foods a smaller person eats. Choosing healthy foods and being active is much more important than being a certain size.

2. Thinness can be unhealthy, too.
    True: Being "under" weight is unhealthy, and just because a person is slim doesn't mean he is healthy. Eating good fruits, vegetables, grains, nuts, and beans, being active (playing outside, participating in sports), getting enough sleep, drinking plenty of water, and having quiet prayer time every day helps a person stay healthy. Whether you were born with a smaller frame or a heavier frame doesn't matter.

3. If you diet and exercise enough, you can look like the people on television and in the magazines.
    False: The people you see on TV and in the movies spend hours having their hair done just right and their make-up applied. Some even have surgery to look thinner or younger. All the unflattering angles (like when an actor's butt looks too big) are edited out. In magazines, photographs are altered to make the women's thighs smaller or the men's muscles bigger. Snip, snip, there goes the model's tummy! It is humanly impossible for a regular person to look like these people. Even celebrities don't look that perfect in real life!

4. There is such a thing as too much exercise.
    True: Too much exercise can be a bad thing! Excessive exercise may be a sign that someone is overly worried about his body size, and can be a sign of an eating disorder.

5. Heavier people must be too lazy to exercise.
    False: The genes that we inherit from our mothers and fathers determine whether or not our bodies are big or small or in-between—not how much time we spend at the gym. Heavier people may exercise just as much as thinner people and even be healthier. God created each person's shape.

Stereotypes

Begin by discussing different media with students, and which senses are engaged: sight, sound, taste, touch, or smell? For example, you listen to music—and if the bass is heavy enough, you can even feel it! Ask students to describe how all five senses are used in eating a meal.

Now think about television. It can't help but be superficial—the main sense involved is sight. The makers of advertisements and TV shows have let you know what to think using pictures. Stereotypes are a simple way to help tell a story, even though they're wrong and hurtful. Have students think of some common stereotypes such as old men are grumpy, girls are bad at math, blondes are dumb, and boys don't cry.

Have students create an imaginary TV show in which the main character, Henry, is supposed to be very smart. How can students let the audience know that Henry is smart? Make him wear glasses? Have him carry lots of books? Wear his pants pulled up to his chest—Urkel style? Ask students to draw pictures of how Henry looks in their minds.

Afterward, look at the drawings together as a class and see if students have relied on stereotypes to create Henry. Do all smart people wear glasses? What other stereotypes are used on TV?

Body image

Man looks at the outward appearance, but the LORD looks at the heart.
1 Samuel 16:7

We tend to think of beauty as an external thing, determined by what a person looks like or what they wear. But of course the best kind of beauty comes from the inside. Ask students to think of the most beautiful person they know (outside of class)—a friend, a coach, a teacher, a neighbor, etc. Have students write a description explaining what makes this person beautiful on the inside and out. Remind students to think about internal qualities such as confidence, sense of humor, maturity, and kindness. Students can share what they've written with the rest of the class.

The perfect body

Have students collect images from magazines that show our culture's ideal man or woman. Students can make a collage from different body parts to create the "perfect" person from head to toe (from shiny ponytail to stylish athletic shoes). Students can write their own words, or glue words from the magazine to describe the ideal people. For example, "tall," "gorgeous," "skinny," or "young."

Afterward, discuss how societies throughout history have defined "beautiful" in many different ways. Divide the class into small groups and assign each group a culture or time period to research. Use these ideas as starting points:

- The Maasai people in Kenya use the same word for "physical beauty" as they do for "character" or "goodness." Traits like bravery, and friendliness make a person "good-looking." Physically, women are admired for their short hair and stretched earlobes, and men are more attractive if they carry a big stick!

- Fashionable Europeans once wore elaborate wigs powdered with flour

- In Cameroon and some other parts of Africa, fat shows prosperity and fertility—especially a fat bottom!

- Until it was outlawed in 1911, having bound feet helped a Chinese woman's social status and marriage prospects.

- Women in 16th century England wore corsets to create a straight torso and flat bust (the hourglass came into style later).

Teasing and bullying

Students may be surprised to learn that Jesus was mocked for eating too much: "The Son of Man came eating and drinking, and they say, 'Here is a glutton...'" (Matthew 11:19). This sort of teasing and ridicule is all too familiar to overweight students. Have students create a no-harassment policy to post in class. Here's a sample outline:

EACH STUDENT IN MR. DELIDES' CLASS IS CREATED IN GOD'S IMAGE. MAKING FUN, BULLYING, OR EVEN SNICKERING ABOUT SOMEONE'S APPEARANCE IS WRONG AND HURTFUL.

1. IF SOMEONE IS BEING TREATED BADLY, THERE ARE NO INNOCENT BYSTANDERS. WE ARE ALL RESPONSIBLE, SO SPEAK UP!

2. TEASERS USUALLY PUT DOWN OTHERS BECAUSE THEY FEEL BAD ABOUT THEMSELVES. DO NOT TRY TO HUMILIATE THE TEASER, BUT TALK TO HIM OR HER ONE-ON-ONE IN A SPIRIT OF LOVE. (2 THESSALONIANS 3:15).

3. LET YOUR CONSCIOUS GUIDE YOU WHETHER OR NOT TO REPORT TEASING OR BULLYING TO MR. DELIDES.

Role-playing

Role-playing exercises can help students learn how to respond to different types of body image situations. Allow students to take turns working out the following scenarios in front of the class. After students have tried a few, allow spectators to raise their hands if they'd like to enter the situation with a different approach. When you feel the scene has played out, announce "cut" to end the action. Allow students to share what they've learned about teasing with younger classes.

1. Two students sit at a lunch table. When one student eats a big cookie, the other makes pig noises.
2. A student watches someone making fun of someone on TV for being short or tall, fat or skinny, etc. (the student(s) playing the TV characters can parody a popular episode or commercial that makes fun of someone for looking a certain way).
3. Three friends are together on the bus. One says something about how ugly she feels with her frizzy hair.
4. A group of students are walking home from school talking about gym class. One makes a comment about a classmate's thighs jiggling when she runs.
5. A student's mother asks him if her butt looks fat.
6. A student's aunt calls him "four eyes" and tells him he'll need to get contacts if he wants a girlfriend.

Name _____

A Matter of the Heart

*Man looks at the outward appearance,
but the Lord looks at the heart.*
1 Samuel 16:7

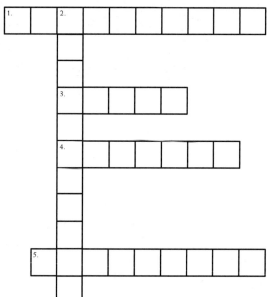

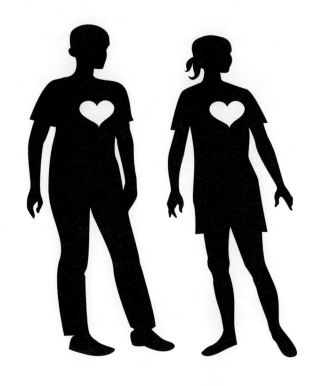

ACROSS

1. An untrue oversimplification about a group of people
3. A reproduction or likeness
4. Someone who eats too much (Jesus was ridiculed for being this)
5. What we think about our own body, regardless of how it looks in reality

DOWN

2. When a person obsesses about food, eating, and body weight to deal with an emotional problem like depression

Answer true or false.

1. _____ Jesus was made fun of for eating too much.

2. _____ Is this stereotype true or false? Boys are bad dancers.

3. _____ Only girls have eating disorders.

4. _____ You can tell someone has anorexia by looking at them—people with anorexia are always really skinny.

5. _____ If everyone else thinks you look good, then you can have a positive body image.

Chapter 5—Nonconforming; proving God's will

. . . offer your bodies as living sacrifices, holy and pleasing to God—this is your spiritual act of worship. Do not conform any longer to the pattern of this world . . . Then you will be able to test and approve what God's will is—his good, pleasing and perfect will.

Romans 12:1-2

Fast food, TV, video games, and the internet are such a part of our world's "pattern" that we don't often think of the dark consequences of these habits—poor nutrition, a sedentary lifestyle, and eventually, disease and death.

We are quick to teach against other forms of toxic behavior—drug abuse, for example—but fail to give our students Bible-based guidance regarding junk food and the boob tube—much more insidious threats to their health. The following activities will help students recognize and resist the world's pattern in their everyday lives, from Saturday morning cartoons to after-dinner chat rooms.

Did you know?

Remind students that things like junk food and TV are not inherently evil. Reflect on 1 Corinthians 9:25 NASB: "Everyone who competes in the games exercises self-control in all things. They do it to receive a perishable wreath [or crown], but we an imperishable." What does it mean to do exercise self-control? Have students think of other things that might be okay in moderation but can become bad habits in excess.

Of course the Bible doesn't mention fast food, and Jesus never condemns couch potatoes. But what is not explicitly addressed in the Bible is abundantly clear in God's other revelation: His Creation. Consider what "God's grocery store," or what He intended us to drink and eat—water, grains, fresh fruits and vegetables. Are we "made" to nourish ourselves with soda or deep-fried potatoes?

Peer pressure has been around since ancient times. In Exodus 23:2, Moses warned the Hebrew people, "Do not follow the crowd in doing wrong."

The Race Against Junk Food by Anthony Buono et al: HCOM Inc., 1997. (Picture book) Tommy and the SNAK posse get kids excited about a healthy lifestyle.

The Berenstain Bears and Too Much TV by Jan Berenstain: Random House, 1984. (Picture book) The Berenstains are spending too much time in front of the television, so Mama Bear bans it for a week. Read to find out if they survive!

It's Disgusting and We Ate It!: True Food Facts from Around the World and Throughout History by James Solheim: Aladdin Library, 2001. (Picture book) Maggots anyone? Be sure to have students try to think objectively about junk food we eat today.

Mrs. Pattern

Materials

Adult volunteer

Pens or soft pencils

Newsprint or paper

Drawing board or something to bear down on

Happy face portrait photocopies

Tape

The following exercise shows just how boring the world's pattern can be. Recruit a parent or other volunteer with a good poker face to play "Mrs. Pattern," a visiting art instructor with odd taste. Mrs. Pattern pairs up students for a lesson in portraiture, but gets frustrated with how different all the portraits are. "Why do you girls and boys have to have such different faces?" she complains. "Big eyes, blue eyes, brown eyes. This boy here has such nice eyes, everyone look at him and draw his eyes. And erase your noses. Everyone draw this girl's nose . . ."

This goes on until Mrs. Pattern, in exasperation, asks everyone to stop drawing and tape their portraits to the wall for a critique. Seeing the variety before her, she throws her hands in the air, "Not two of them are identical!"

Mrs. Pattern announces that students must repeat the exercise—except this time, the portraits will be neat and regular and uniform. Mrs. Pattern hands out the portrait happy face photocopy (see page 57) and instructs students to color it—not just any color they choose, however—only yellow.

Finally, declare that Mrs. Pattern is just to show how boring the world would be if everything looked the same. Share Psalm 139 with students, and talk about how God created each person to be unique. What are the physical differences they see in all the different portraits? What about each person's strengths and gifts—is one student a talented singer? Is another great at sports? Have each student share with the class one thing that makes their portrait partner special.

You know me inside and out, you know every bone in my body;
You know exactly how I was made, bit by bit, how I was sculpted from nothing into something.
Like an open book, you watched me grow from conception to birth; all the stages of my life were spread out before you,
The days of my life all prepared before I'd even lived one day.
Your thoughts—how rare, how beautiful! God, I'll never comprehend them!
Psalm 139:15-17 THE MESSAGE

Happy Face Patterns

Copy and cut out a happy face pattern for each child. Use with the Mrs. Pattern activity on page 56.

Just say no thank you

Even though a poor diet is as hazardous to a person's health as smoking, pigging out on super-sized fries is still more socially acceptable. A Houston church even opened a McDonald's® on their property to make eating "more convenient for children!" What's next, a kids' smoking lounge to take the hassle out of lighting up? Have students research the health effects of smoking compared to a diet high in sugar and saturated fat. The National Center for Tobacco-Free Kids and the Centers for Disease Control are great places to start [the sources for the following statistics]. As the following sample statistics demonstrate, the similarities are alarming.

 5.5 billion dollars is spent by the tobacco industry each year marketing its products.

 12 billion dollars is spent each year on advertising targeted at children—about half is for fast food, sugary cereals, soda, and candy.

 Kids consume 900 million packs of cigarettes each year.

 "Billions and billions" have been served at McDonald's alone.

 17% of kids under 18 are smokers.

 13% of kids under 18 are in very poor health because of too little exercise and eating unhealthy foods.

 Smoking makes it harder to run and to play sports.

 Being out of shape makes it harder to run and to play sports.

 Tobacco users are at risk for many health problems including heart disease, stroke, and some types of cancer.

 People who regularly eat foods high in sugar and saturated fat are at risk for many health problems including heart disease, stroke, and some types of cancer.

 400,00 people die each year from their own smoking.

 300,000 people die each year from poor nutrition and physical inactivity.

Class-health report card

Use the point system to determine how healthy the class is as a whole. Students may wish to suggest other activities that they believe should qualify for "checks" (for example, going to the gym with Mom, walking the dog, choosing a healthy after school snack, etc.) How many checks do most students have? (Advanced classes can calculate the mean and average.) Explain that students should do their best to get at least 3 checks.

_____ I get home by walking or biking.

_____ I participate in sports, dance lessons, or another athletic activity several times a week.

_____ I spend time playing outside almost every day.

_____ I eat dinner with the TV off.

_____ I limit TV, video games, talking on the phone, and Internet use to one hour each night.

No junking

Students can use the facts they've discovered to create posters for the classroom and cafeteria. Use the following ideas to get kids started.

Choose fruit, veggies, nuts, and other healthy foods over pre-packaged snacks.

Give a cold cup of water to these little ones (Matthew 10:42)—not soda, a sports beverage, Sunny D®, or Kool-Aid®!

Help make this a junk-free environment. Eat whole foods from God's grocery store!

After school planner

Scheduling can help students make the most out of their time at home after school. Remind students to include activities such as lessons or practices, snack time, homework, dinner, TV, video games, Internet, quiet time, etc.

Allow students to take a few minutes toward the end of the school day to plan their schedules for the upcoming evening. Use the following sample as a guide:

Name: Erin
Today is: Tuesday

3:PM: Soccer Practice After School from 3:15 to 4:00
4:PM: Get Home at 4:30 and Have a Snack
5:PM: Ride Bikes with Camron until dinner.
6:PM: Eat Dinner at 6:00
7:PM: Do Homework from 7:00 to 7:30, Then
        Spend About 15 Minutes Checking Email.
8:PM: Watch Angelina Ballerina (taped from Saturday)
9:PM: Have Quiet Time, Then Lights out.

Do students think the schedule might be useful? Discuss how planning can help students avoid wasting too much time flipping channels or chatting on the Internet. Seeing it written down, do students see any changes they'd like to make—for instance, making more room for quiet time?

Videotaping programs ahead of time is a great way to manage children's viewing time, and it encourages family interaction by allowing pauses for discussion.

Wal-Mart, Wal-Mart®, everywhere . . .

Frozen fruit juice pops and bran muffins are great (and nutritious) examples of patterns. Prepare these treats in class, and point out how the mold makes everything the same shape.

FROZEN FRUIT POPS

Papaya juice
Cranberry juice
Molds or paper cups and craft sticks

Fill each mold halfway up with papaya juice and freeze until firm, about an hour. Fill the rest of the mold with cranberry juice, insert toothpicks, and freeze until very hard. Remove the fruit pop from the mold and cool down with this healthy, refreshing treat.

Invent your own favorite combinations with different juices, pureed fruit, yogurt, milk, honey, or whatever is on hand.

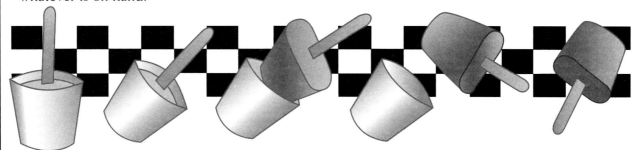

APPLE BRAN MUFFINS

1 cup wheat bran
1 cup unbleached all-purpose flour
1 ²/₃ cup whole-wheat flour
2 teaspoon ground cinnamon
1 teaspoon baking soda
2 cups skim milk

4 teaspoons lemon juice
2 egg whites
1 cup plus 2 tablespoons molasses
1 tablespoons olive oil
1 teaspoon vanilla extract
1 large, sweet apple, unpeeled, coarsely shredded (1 cup)

Combine bran, both types of flour, cinnamon, and baking soda in a large bowl. Mix well. In a medium bowl, combine milk and lemon juice. Let stand 1 minute. Add remaining ingredients, except apple. Beat with a fork or wire whisk until blended. Stir in apple. Add to dry mixture, mixing until all dry ingredients are moistened. Refrigerate until baking time. Preheat oven to 375°. Lightly oil 12 muffin cups or spray with nonstick cooking spray. Divide mixture evenly into muffin cups. Bake 20 to 25 minutes, until a toothpick inserted into the center of a muffin comes out clean. Remove muffins to a rack to cool.

Low-tech demonstration

Use a cookie cutter to shape slices of whole grain bread and cheese for sandwiches during snack time. While children are snacking, ask them to think about the phrase "the pattern of this world." What in the world is like a cookie cutter, muffin pan, or fruit pop tray? How are we "molded" by TV, advertisements, movies, and the web?

Have students name a few national clothing stores. Can you get the same pair of jeans in any mall in America? What about what we eat? Ask if any students have been to a chain restaurant in another state—was the food pretty much exactly the same? What about how we entertain ourselves? Do we all watch the same movies, listen to the same songs, and watch the same TV shows?

What's the downside of all this sameness? First of all, it's just plain boring. Who wants to eat a hamburger everyday when God created such a variety of plants and foods in different places? Also, we've all been given different gifts to develop (1 Corinthians 12:4), like music, art, dancing, athletics, etc. These gifts may go to waste if everybody spends their free time playing the same video game!

Prove It!

Share the verses below with children. Explain that when it comes to popular culture, God wants His children to be non-conformists!

Do not be conformed to this world (this age), [fashioned after and adapted to its external, superficial customs]. . . .
Romans 12:2 AMP

Don't become so well-adjusted to your culture that you fit into it without even thinking.
Romans 12:2

The Greek word "conform" or suschematizo (soos-khay-mat-id'-zo), that is used in Romans 12:1-2 means "to conform one's self (i.e. one's mind and character) to another's pattern." If we are not to conform to this world or our culture, what are we to conform to?

Instead, fix your attention on God. You'll be changed from the inside out. Readily recognize what he wants from you, and quickly respond to it. Unlike the culture around you, always dragging you down to its level of immaturity, God brings the best out of you, develops well-formed maturity in you.
Romans 12:2 THE MESSAGE

What happens when we fix our attention on God and conform our lives to His Word?

Then you will be able to test and approve what God's will is—his good, pleasing and perfect will.
Romans 12:2

No Sponge Bob Square Pants? Now that's a sacrifice!

Again, the kingdom of heaven is like a merchant looking for fine pearls.
When he found one of great value, he went away an sold everything he had and bought it.

Matthew 13:45-46

When we think of the word "sacrifice" (Romans 12:1-2), we tend to focus on what we're giving up—but Jesus thought of sacrifice in terms of gain. Remind students of the spiritual gains that come along with any sacrifice to do what is right: approval of God, respect from friends and family, triumph over our moral enemy, increased self-control, and greater usefulness to serve others.

Have students think of some sacrifices they would like to make in order to take better care of their bodies. Have them list the sacrifice on the left-hand side of a sheet of paper, and then list all they would have to gain on the right side.

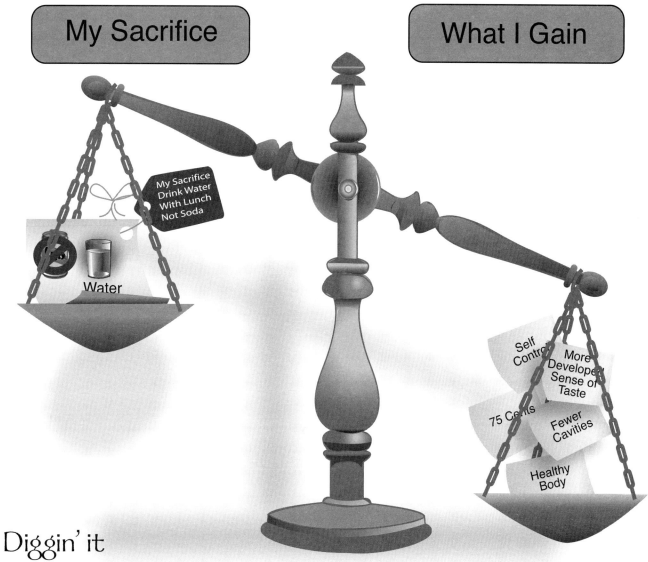

Diggin' it

Give students a new perspective on our TV culture. Allow students to read, rehearse, and then perform the skit on pages 64-65. Afterward, discuss what sort of things would be "evidence" of Christianity. Remind students that our legacy doesn't have to be left behind in a landfill—preserving God's creation and sharing the good news with others is a better legacy.

Skit: Diggin' It

Props
> Television
> One copy of TV Guide
> Burger wrapper with golden arches

Characters
> Students 1, 2, 3, and 4
> Professor

Student 1: We've made a discovery, professor! I believe it's almost 3,000 years old—from the year 2005.

> *Student 1 uncovers a television, and the other students gasp with amazement.*

Professor: *(examining the television)* Interesting, very interesting. Who can tell me what this is?

Student 2: It obviously has religious importance. Maybe it's an idol?

Professor: What makes you think that?

Student 2: Well, just look at where we found it. All the furniture in the room points toward it, and it's in front of these altar-like seats—I think they called it, um…a crouch?

Student 3: Couch, they were called couches. From the French word couchiér: to lay down. *(Grins smugly, other students roll their eyes.)*

Professor: What do you mean by altar?

Student 2: The seats were soft and comfortable, so that they could sit for hours before the Box, probably in a trance state.

Student 3: Yes, a trance—a dazed, hypnotic condition recorded in the worship practices of the Vodun, or Voodoo peoples of West Africa in the 18th century . . .

Student 2: As I was saying, the seats are comfortable so that people could sit for long periods of time while worshipping this object.

> *Student 4 notices a TV Guide behind the television and delicately holds it up for everyone to see:*

Student 4: I found some sort of book!

Student 2: Perhaps it's some type of scripture—a collection of sacred writings.

Student 4: *(opens the TV Guide and reads aloud)* Saturday, 8 o'clock, Hey Arnold!...8:30, Little Bill, 9 o'clock, Dora the Explorer... It goes on and on, every hour of every day. Is it some sort of worship schedule?

Student 1: Oh, so they weren't worshipping the Box itself, they were worshipping pictures of people on this screen. Arnold, Little Bill, and Dora must have been their gods.

Student 2: But professor, I thought the most common religion in this part of the world in the year 2005 was Christianity?

Professor: Yes, we used to think so. But overwhelming evidence has disproved that theory.

Student 3: *(raises his or her hand eagerly)* Precisely, Professor. The most important structures in 2005 were consumer-oriented. *(condescendingly to other students)* Places for people to buy stuff. Wal-Mart's® parking lot alone was bigger than most churches.

Professor: Let me tell you a little bit about the Box. It was actually known as a "television" *(to Student 3)* —from the French télévision—and it was just a minor object of worship. The people of 2005 worshipped another god. We have billions and billions of relics from all over the world—monuments, literature, even little objects that appear to be toys. Garbage dumps are full of artifacts just like this one *(The professor holds up a burger wrapper adorned with Golden Arches)*. The true religion of 2005 was most certainly McDonaldism.

Prove It!

. . . offer your bodies as living sacrifices, holy and pleasing to God—this is your spiritual act of worship. Do not conform any longer to the pattern of this world . . . Then you will be able to test and approve what God's will is—his good, pleasing and perfect will.

Romans 12:1-2

Now that you have learned about nutrition and fitness, find out about the responsibility you have by finishing the the verse below. Unscramble the words and then fill in the coded letters.

a model to copy	N A T R T E P	_ _ _ _ _ _ _ 13 4
to become like other people	N O M F R O C	_ _ _ _ _ _ _
a frame that shapes something	D O L M	_ _ _ _ 8 1
to give up something	F R E A I I S C C	_ _ _ _ _ _ _ _ _ 5 7 10 9
to be in charge over your own actions	L E F S - R T O L C N O	_ _ _ _-_ _ _ _ _ _ _ 12 6 3 2 11

AS OBEDIENT CHILDREN, _ _   _ _ _   _ _ _ _ _ _ _   _ _
                        1 2   3 2 4   5 2 3 6 2 7 8   4 2

_ **H** _   _ **V** _ _   _ _ _ _ _ _ _   **Y** _ **U**   **H** _ _
4   9   9   10 11   1 9 12 10 7 9 12   2   13 1

W H _ _   **Y** _ **U**   _ _ **V** _   _ _   _ **G** _ _ _ _ _ _ .
9 3   2   11 10   9 1   10 3   10   3 2 7 13 3 5 9

1 PETER 1:14

 CD-204008 *Taking Godly Care of My Body*

Chapter 6:—World health

For I was hungry and you gave me something to eat, I was thirsty and you gave me something to drink . . .
I was sick and you looked after me . . . "whatever you did for one of the least of these brothers of mine, you did for me."
Matthew 25:35-40

In these verses, Jesus tells us that whenever we care for someone in need, it's as if we are doing it for Jesus Himself. The health of "the least of these brothers of mine" should concern us just as much as our own health. In this chapter, students can take what they've learned about body stewardship and use it to help their neighbor—whether that means a retirement community down the street or a hungry village across the world.

Did you know?

Who does Jesus mean by "the least of these"? Ask students to think of the people that our culture thinks the "least" of. Who are the least powerful? Why are poor, sick, elderly, or disabled people treated badly sometimes?

In 1 Timothy 4:8 we learn that "Physical training is of some value, but godliness has value for all things." Have students think about the two parts of this verse. First, it tells us that physical training, or exercise, is valuable—but godliness, or loving God, is the most important thing.

Take Action! A Guide to Active Citizenship by Craig and Marc Kielburger: John Wiley & Sons, 2002. (Non-fiction) Step-by-step instructions for students wanting to make a difference in their hometown or the world.

If Jesus Came to My House by Joan G. Thomas: HarperCollins, 1951. (Picture book) Instead of asking "What would Jesus do?," ask, "If Jesus were here, what would I do?"

Jesus was here?

Materials:
> Photos of people in need from magazines or newspapers

How would students behave if Jesus were visiting your classroom today? If He were hungry or thirsty, they would probably fall over each other fetching water or deciding who got to share her lunch with Him.

Inform students that Jesus is present in our world today—we can actually see Him, touch Him, hear Him, and even smell Him! Inform students that you have proof—an actual photograph. Pass around the photographs of people in need, and ask students to figure out which one is Jesus. For a hint, tell them they can look up Matthew 25:31-46.

Discuss how sick people, hungry people, and anyone else in need is like Jesus Himself. And whenever we care for them, it's just like we are doing it for Jesus Himself!

I have neighbors in Zambia?

Instruct students to draw their next-door neighbors' house and connect their house to it. For example, a student could draw a house and label it "Schwartz family."

Next, instruct students to draw smaller houses connected to their house representing all the other neighbors who they know. When students have written down every last one of their neighbors, ask them to think about whom they consider a "neighbor." Did they only include people who live in the same street? Within walking distance?

Inform students that Jesus gave us a totally different definition for neighbor. To find it, read the story of the traveling Samaritan (Luke 10:25-37). Our neighbor is anyone who is in need, not necessarily someone who lives nearby. We are called to be good neighbors and show mercy to people in need all over the world!

Using a globe or world map, point out where some of the world's poorest people live—most of them don't live in North America. Remind students that the people who live there are our neighbors, too. Divide students into groups and have each group select a country. Let them get to know their new neighbors using an almanac, the library, or the web. What languages do the people speak? What's the flag look like? What's the country's history? What health issues do the people face (AIDS, malaria, malnutrition, etc.)? What's the average life expectancy?

No funnel cake?

Students can share what they've learned in the first five chapters with the school by hosting a health fair.

Booth ideas:

- Five booths, each features fruit, vegetables, whole grains, nuts, or beans and legumes . . . samples provided

- Learn to measure your heart rate

- Students perform the *Diggin' It* skit from pages 64-65

- Students lead audience in song and dance from page 41

- Students distribute maps of area walking or biking trails

- Student-made charts to compare smoking with a poor diet

Get moving!

Help students turn their awareness into action. Encourage everyone to be on the lookout for health and human rights issues in their hometown and far away—anything that doesn't feel fair that they'd like to do something about.

First step:
Identify a problem

Students can learn about a need by reading the newspaper or asking parents. Give students a week to identify different issues then allow them to share their findings with the class.

Here are a few places to start:

- Sponsor an AIDS orphanage
- Do Meals on Bike Wheels for a few people who live near the school
- Help residents of a retirement community be active
- Raise money for measles vaccinations in a high-risk area
- Assist a community member with medical expenses
- Partner with an underprivileged school for mentoring or tutoring

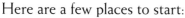

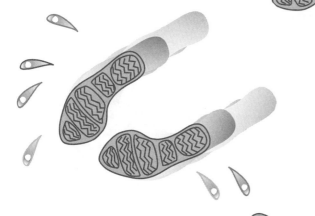

Second step:
Select one issue

Guide the class in choosing one issue to learn about in detail, or nominate a few and allow students to vote.

Third step:
Get specific

Narrow the scope of the project to a manageable size. For example, if students want to help the residents of a retirement community be active, the goal could be small (doing movement songs with the residents one day) or larger (planting a garden for residents to help tend).

Fourth step:
Hit the books

Once students have chosen an issue, encourage them to find out as much as possible about the problem. (Which countries have high rates of measles? How many children die from measles each year? How much does the vaccine cost?) Assign small groups specific research topics and class presentations.

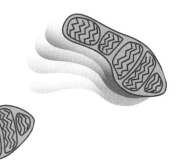

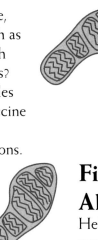
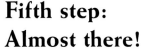

Fifth step:
Almost there!

Help students figure out how to meet their goals. Create a timeline. Plan fund-raising or letter writing objectives.

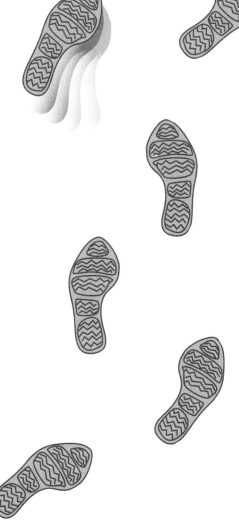

Sixth step:
On your marks, get set...Go!

Now it's time for the fun part! Make the calls, collect supplies, and remind students to keep supporters informed of their progress. Celebrate steps that bring the class closer to its final goal.

World health problems can sometimes seem overwhelming; even to students determined to make a difference. Remind everyone of Matthew 17:20: "Nothing will be impossible for you." Whether they want to help a community member with their doctor bills or wipe out malaria in Madagascar, "All things are possible with God." (Mark 10:27)

Hikathon

A walkathon or hikathon at a local park is a great way for students to raise money and show their commitment to fitness. Follow this outline to put the fun in fund raising. Use the funds to show love to your neighbors. Start by assigning team and individual responsibilities:

Mechanics team: set date and place, map course, coordinate event day volunteers

Registration team: keep track of sign-up sheets, contact walkers with event information

Accounting team: receive entry donations and pledges

Flyer team: design and post flyers around school and town

Publicity team: contact local news media

Sponsorship team: solicit beverages, snacks, t-shirts and other donations from area businesses

Pledge forms and flyers

Encourage students to request support from their families, neighbors, and churches. Use the samples below to plan your own pledge forms and flyers. Provide students with extra copies for others who want to join the walkathon.

HIKATHON FOR HUNGER
JOIN MR. PETROV'S 4TH GRADERS IN FIGHTING HUNGER!

All proceeds benefit Marydale Senior Center's senior meals program for the Shawnee River Tribes where over 47% of area seniors live alone and below the poverty line.

Pledger's name: _____

Student's name: _____

Amount pledged: $_____ or _____ per mile

PUT ON YOUR SNEAKERS FOR
WESLEYAN CHRISTIAN ACADEMY'S

HIKATHON FOR HUNGER

A TEAM EVENT TO BENEFIT
THE SENIOR MEALS PROGRAM OF THE SHAWNEE RIVER TRIBES

Walk a mile in Grandma's orthopedics!
* Over 47% of area seniors live alone and below the poverty line
When: Saturday, October 16th, 8 A.M.
Where: Evergreen Park

$5 donation to enter
For more information or to sponsor a student, call 555-8769

Hikathon 555-8769 Hikathon 555-8769 Hikathon 555-8769 Hikathon 555-8769 Hikathon 555-8769

CD-204008 *Taking Godly Care of My Body*

More fund-raising fun

 Students can continue the lessons in Chapter 2 (Our daily bread) by having a healthy bake sale with bran muffins, whole wheat bread, oatmeal cookies, and whole grain treats.

 Curtain! Perform a play or the skit from Chapter 5 (*Diggin' It*, page 64) before an audience and charge admission.

 Organize a car wash for parents after school.

 Recycle aluminum cans, paper, or ink cartridges.

 Allow students to buy and sell singing telegrams to deliver to classmates.

 Sell raffle tickets. Solicit local businesses for a donated prize, and all the profits can go toward the aid project.

 Run a healthy snacks stand during school or at school events. Fruits, veggies, and nuts are good for you, and inexpensive enough so that even a moderate markup creates great profits.

 Organize a gift-wrapping service for parents after school in December.

Disciple detectives

Can you tell if someone is a Christian just by looking? Jesus tells us in John 13:34 that we can tell who His disciples are by an outward sign. Can students figure out what the sign is?

Read the true/false statements to the class so they can detect the disciple of Jesus.

1. Disciples of Jesus eat healthy foods.
2. Disciples of Jesus get enough exercise.
3. Disciples of Jesus are good at video games.
4. Disciples of Jesus always do their homework.
5. Disciples of Jesus pray.
6. Disciples of Jesus give to their church.
7. Disciples of Jesus are good at sports.
8. Disciples of Jesus love and serve other people.

As a class, talk about the pictures on this page and why or why not students think the characters are Jesus' disciples. Finally, inform students that only the last statement, number eight, shows the outward sign Jesus talks about. Students can look up John 13:34 for proof.

A new command I give you: Love one another. As I have loved you, so you must love one another. By this all men will know that you are my disciples, if you love one another.

John 13:34

Explain to students that disciples can go to church, eat healthy foods, exercise, etc., but Jesus tells us one sure way to show that we're Christians: to serve and love others like He did.

The dirty feet award

Read John 13 and discover what it means to love Jesus' way. How did Jesus show perfect love, the greatest love of all? With a brilliant sermon? A heavenly display of fireworks?

Have students read John 13:1-17 to find out. Jesus showed us how to love by washing His disciples' feet! Ask students to imagine how dirty and blistered their feet were—walking in the dust all day in sandals, with sand, mud, animal droppings, and sharp rocks! Only servants or slaves would have had such a nasty job.

Since we wear socks and shoes today, what are other yucky chores we can do for others? Ask each student to think of one gross chore they can do for homework. Students can report back in the morning, and the most creative description wins a prize. For fun, give the winner a bar of soap or an all day washroom pass along with the certificate.

Icky ideas:
>   Changing your baby sister's diaper
>   Cleaning your grandma's toilet
>   Hand washing your little brother's underwear
>   Picking up litter
>   Cleaning your dog's ears

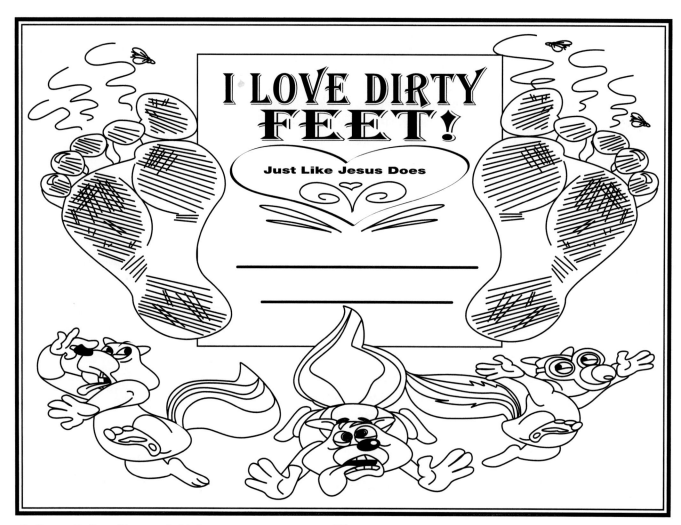

Name_____

All You Need Is Love

Did you know that the whole Bible can be summed up in five words? Use the picture codes to find out what Jesus said sums up everything! Afterward, think of ways you can follow this command.

THE ENTIRE LAW IS SUMMED UP IN A SINGLE COMMAND:

"

"

   .

GALATIANS 5:14

♡ = Y   🦋 = U   🕯 = I

⟨)(= E   ◊ = L   🕊 = N

📖 = O   🌼 = R   ☀ = H

🌾 = B   🏛 = V   (head) = G

$ = A   🌙 = F   ♻ = S

Scripture Index

Chapter 1—It's my body! (Or, is it?)

Do you not know that your body is a temple of the Holy Spirit, who is in you, whom you have received from God? You are not your own; you were bought at a price. Therefore honor God with your body. 1 Corinthians 6:19-20

The earth is the LORD's, and everything in it, the world, and all who live in it. . . . Psalm 24:1

If I take part in the meal with thankfulness, why am I denounced because of something I thank God for? So whether you eat or drink or whatever you do, do it all for the glory of God. 1 Corinthians 10:30-31

. . . God created [food] to be received with thanksgiving by those who believe and who know the truth. For everything God created is good, and nothing is to be rejected if it is received with thanksgiving, because it is consecrated by the word of God and prayer. 1 Timothy 4:3-5

A cheerful heart is good medicine, but a crushed spirit dries up the bones. Proverbs 17:22

I will meditate on all your works and consider all your mighty deeds. Psalm 77:12

I remember the days of long ago; I meditate on all your works and consider what your hands have done. Psalm 143:5

"Be still, and know that I am God. . . ." Psalm 46:10

Passages: Matthew 25:14-30, Matthew 6:16-18, 1 Kings 19:11-13

Chapter 2—Our daily bread

Give us today our daily bread. Matthew 6:11

He will eat curds and honey when he knows enough to reject the wrong and choose the right. Isaiah 7:15

Even my close friend, whom I trusted, he who shared my bread, has lifted up his heel against me. Psalm 41:9

There is a way that seems right to a man, but in the end it leads to death. Proverbs 14:12

Whatever is good and perfect comes to us from God above, who created all heaven's lights. Unlike them, he never changes or casts shifting shadows. James 1:17 NLT

For the LORD your God is bringing you into a good land—a land with streams and pools of water, with springs flowing in the valleys and hills; a land with wheat and barley, vines and fig trees, pomegranates, olive oil and honey. . . . Deuteronomy 8:7-8

Laughter and bread go together. Ecclesiastes 10:19 THE MESSAGE

[Early Christians] devoted themselves to the apostles' teaching and to the fellowship, to the breaking of bread and to prayer. . . . They broke bread in their homes and ate together with glad and sincere hearts. Acts 2:42,46

On a certain Sabbath Jesus was walking through a field of ripe grain. His disciples were pulling off heads of grain, rubbing them in their hands to get rid of the chaff, and eating them. Luke 6:1 THE MESSAGE

If you enter your neighbor's grainfield, you may pick kernels with your hands, but you must not put a sickle to his standing grain. Deuteronomy 23:25

Even the stork in the sky knows her appointed seasons, and the dove, the swift and the thrush observe the time of their migration. But my people do not know the requirements of the LORD. Jeremiah 8:7

"But ask the animals, and they will teach you, or the birds of the air, and they will tell you; or speak to the earth, and it will teach you, or let the fish of the sea inform you." Job 12:7-8

. . . cannot my taste discern perverse things? Job 6:30 KJV

But solid food is for the mature, who because of practice have their senses trained to discern good and evil. Hebrews 5:14 NASB

[God] puts the best bread on your tables. Psalm 147:14 THE MESSAGE

. . . the valleys are carpeted with grain. They all shout and sing for joy! Psalm 65:13, NLT

Passage: Exodus 16

Chapter 3—All your strength

"Love the Lord your God with all your heart and with all your soul and with all your mind and with all your strength." Mark 12:30

"By the sweat of your brow you will eat your food. . . ." Genesis 3:19

. . . praise him with tambourine and dancing. . . . Psalm 150:4

Then Miriam the prophetess, Aaron's sister, took a tambourine in her hand, and all the women followed her, with tambourines and dancing. Exodus 15:20

David . . . danced before the Lord with all his might. . . . 2 Samuel 6:14

I will exalt you, O Lᴏʀᴅ, for you lifted me out of the depths and did not let my enemies gloat over me. Psalm 30:1

[Jesus] rejoiced greatly in the Holy Spirit. . . . Luke 10:21 ɴᴀsʙ

The jailer brought them into his house and set a meal before them; he was filled with joy because he had come to believe in God—he and his whole family. Acts 16:34

"Rejoice and be glad, because great is your reward in heaven. . . ." Matthew 5:12

"Therefore my heart is glad and my tongue rejoices; my body also will live in hope. . . ." Acts 2:26

"In God's presence I'll dance all I want! . . . Oh yes, I'll dance to God's glory—more recklessly even than this. And as far as I'm concerned . . . I'll gladly look like a fool. . . ." 2 Samuel 6:21-22 ᴛʜᴇ ᴍᴇssᴀɢᴇ

Let them praise his name with dancing. . . . Psalm 149:3

I love you, O Lᴏʀᴅ, my strength. Psalm 18:1

"But ask the animals, and they will teach you, or the birds of the air, and they will tell you; or speak to the earth, and it will teach you, or let the fish of the sea inform you." Job 12:7-8

Passage: Psalm 150

Chapter 4—Created in Whose image?

I praise you because I am fearfully and wonderfully made. . . . Psalm 139:14

Above all else, guard your heart, for it is the wellspring of life. Proverbs 4:23

"You shall have no other gods before me." Exodus 20:3

Charm is deceptive, and beauty is fleeting; but a woman who fears the Lᴏʀᴅ is to be praised. Proverbs 31:30

"Man looks at the outward appearance, but the Lᴏʀᴅ looks at the heart." 1 Samuel 16:7

The Son of Man came eating and drinking, and they say, 'Here is a glutton. . . .'" Matthew 11:19

Chapter 5—Nonconforming; proving God's will

Therefore, I urge you, brothers, in view of God's mercy, to offer your bodies as living sacrifices, holy and pleasing to God—this is your spiritual act of worship. Do not conform any longer to the pattern of this world, but be transformed by the renewing of your mind. Then you will be able to test and approve what God's will is—his good, pleasing and perfect will. Romans 12:1-2

Everyone who competes in the games exercises self-control in all things. They then do it to receive a perishable wreath, but we an imperishable. 1 Corinthians 9:25 ɴᴀsʙ

"Do not follow the crowd in doing wrong." Exodus 23:2

"And if anyone gives even a cup of cold water to one of these little ones because he is my disciple, I tell you the truth, he will certainly not lose his reward." Matthew 10:42

There are different kinds of gifts, but the same Spirit. 1 Corinthians 12:4

"Again, the kingdom of heaven is like a merchant looking for fine pearls. When he found one of great value, he went away and sold everything he had and bought it." Matthew 13:45-46

As obedient children, do not conform to the evil desires you had when you lived in ignorance. 1 Peter 1:14

Passage: Psalm 139

Chapter 6—World Health

For I was hungry and you gave me something to eat, I was thirsty and you gave me something to drink, I was a stranger and you invited me in, I needed clothes and you clothed me, I was sick and you looked after me, I was in prison and you came to visit me." Matthew 25:35-36

For physical training is of some value, but godliness has value for all things. . . . 1 Timothy 4:8

"Nothing will be impossible for you." Matthew 17:20

All things are possible with God. Mark 10:27

"A new command I give you: Love one another. As I have loved you, so you must love one another. By this all men will know that you are my disciples, if you love one another." John 13:34-35

The entire law is summed up in a single command: "Love your neighbor as yourself. Galatians 5:14

Passages: Matthew 25:31-46, Luke 10:25-37, John 13:1-17

Answer Key

Page 16
Answers will vary.

Page 20

Across
4. honor
6. temple

Down
1. whisper
2. pray
3. fast
5. meditate

Page 27
Wheat kernel should be labeled (top to bottom) bran, endosperm, germ
1. whole wheat
2. the whole kernel: bran, endosperm, and germ
3. minerals, fiber, vitamins, protein, carbohydrate
4. If you enter your neighbor's grainfield, you may pick kernels with your hands.

Page 30
Answers will vary.

Page 36

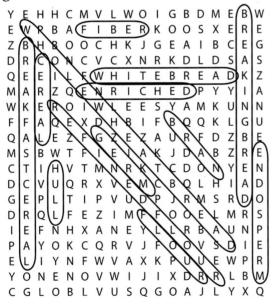

Page 44

Across
3. agalliao
4. strength

Down
1. Jehovah Chezeq
2. dance

Page 48
Answers will vary.

Page 54

Across
1. stereotype
3. image
4. glutton
5. body image

Down
2. eating disorder

1-true, 2-false, 3-false, 4-false, 5-false

Page 66
1. pattern
2. conform
3. mold
4. sacrifice
5. self-control

"As obedient children, do not conform to the evil desires you had when you lived in ignorance."

Page 77
"Love your neighbor as yourself."